Keep it simple and strong

문박사와 천박사의 English Conversation

영문학박사 **문영수** 사회언어학박사 **천재윤** 공저

*Maximize your English with practical English conversation.
*Practise situations in different contexts.

BAEKSAN Publishing Co

Preface

2012년 한 해가 시작된 지도 며칠 흘렀다. 지난해는 국·내외적으로 많은 변화가 있었던 시기였다. 세계정세는 급박하게 돌아갔고 국내적으로는 북측의 변화에 주목해야 했다. 또한 올해는 국가에 중요한 선거가 있는 해이다. 이처럼 변화의 물결은 우리 곁에서 지속적으로 손짓하고 있다.

한 해를 새롭게 맞이하는 시점에서 저자들이 새롭게 준비한 *문박사와 천박사의 English Conversation*을 출판하게 되어 참으로 기쁘다. 본 著書는 영어회화에 초점을 맞춘 책으로 알아두면 유용한 숙어표현을 시작으로 일상 영어회화와 관광 영어회화로 구성되어 있다. 특히 본 著書는 해외여행을 계획하는 여행자뿐만 아니라 관광관련 전공을 하는 대학생들에게 최적의 책으로 자리매김할 것이다. 또한 대학 교양 영어 회화교재로도 널리 활용될 수 있으리라 생각된다. 끝으로 독자들의 많은 발전이 있기를 진심으로 바라는 바이다.

새해벽두에 영문학박사 **문영수**

사회언어학박사 **천재윤**

Contents

I. 문박사와 천박사의 영어회화 2배로 늘려주는 표현

영어회화를 학습하는데 있어 기본적으로 알아두면 도움이 될 만한 표현들을 정리해보았다. 이러한 표현들은 따로 정리해서 익숙해지도록 연습해야 한다. 보다 폭넓은 표현들을 학습하기 위해서는 천재윤(2006)의 술술 내려 읽는 미국영어를 참조하면 된다.

01. He broke up with her.
그는 그녀와 절교했다.

02. He has had a traffic accident.
교통사고가 났다.

03. That's too steep for me.
값이 너무 비싸다.

04. Chances are slim.
가능성이 희박하다.

05. Let's give her a big hand.
박수갈채를 보내자.

06. It doesn't ring a bell.
생각이 나지 않아.

07. It's better than nothing.
없는 것보다 낫다.

08. I'll have the same.
같은 것으로 주세요.

09. I'm positive.
정말 그래.

10. They are neck and neck.
그들은 막상막하다.

11. It takes two to tango.
손바닥도 부딪혀야 소리가 나.

12. It's a pretty short notice.
너무 갑작스런 부탁이다.

13. My lips are sealed.
난 입이 무거운 사람이다.

14. I've had enough.
많이 먹었어.

15. They're selling like a hot cake.
불티나게 팔려.

16. You can say that again.
정말 그래.

17. Lunch is on me.
점심은 내가 살게.

18. Just my luck!
난 운이 없어.

19. It's just a pipe dream.
헛된 망상이다.

20. You read my mind!
내 마음을 잘 아는구나.

21. It slipped my mind.
깜박했다.

22. It's a small world.
세상 좁구나.

23. To you and me!
너와 나를 위해.

24. Why don't you join us for a drink?
같이 한 잔 하자.

25. Are you free tomorrow?
내일 시간 있으세요?

26. How can I get in touch with her?
그녀와 어떻게 연락을 할 수 있지?

27. Did you have a good day today?
오늘 즐거웠니?

28. He'll be with you in a second.
곧 바꿔드릴게요.

29. Can you come down a little?
좀 깎아주세요.

30. That's a pain in the neck.
지겨워.

31. I haven't had a bite since morning.
아침부터 굶었다.

32. It has a smooth ride.
승차감이 좋다.

33. I'm speechless.
말문이 막힌다.

34. I'm not myself today.
오늘 몸이 안 좋다.

35. There is no free lunch.
세상엔 공짜가 없다.

36. Just bring yourself.
그냥 오세요.

37. Keep your nose out of this!
참견하지 마.

38. That's life.
사는 게 다 그래.

39. You're an angel!
정말 고마워요.

40. This year really went by fast.
올해 정말 빨리 지나갔다.

II. 문박사와 천박사의 유용한 숙어표현

이 번장에서는 숙어가 포함된 실용 기본 문장을 학습해보자. 이러한 표현을 잘 숙지해서 사용한다면 의사소통의 묘미를 느낄 수 있다. 보다 세밀한 학습을 원하는 독자는 문영수 · 천재윤(2011)의 English Heritage for Idioms, Collocations and Phrasal Verbs를 참조하기 바란다.

01. I see it's a sore spot for her.

* a sore spot(point, place) 아픈데, 급소, 약점

02. She is as blind as a bat without her glasses.

* as blind as a bat 눈이 먼

03. He has been as busy as a bee these days.

* as busy as a bee 매우 바쁜

04. She felt like a fish out of water.

* like a fish out of water 어색한, 불편한

05. They were caught in the act.

* be caught in the act 현장에서 붙잡히다.

06. Act your age.

* act your age 철들다.

07. I don't mind helping, but I draw the line at doing everything myself.

* draw the line 선을 긋다.

08. It's a long story to tell you.

* a long story 긴 이야기

09. Well, to cut a long story short, he was born as a criminal.

* to cut a long story short 짧게 말하면

10. My teacher is always on my back about doing my assignment on time.

* be on someone's back 계속 요구하다.

11. You scratch my back and I'll scratch yours.

* scratch my back and I'll scratch yours 서로 돕다.

12. Although he's friendly to your face, I suspect he'd stab you in the back.

* stab someone in the back 배신하다.

13. Our ambitious plan is on the back burner now.

* be on the back burner 보류하다.

14. We human have purpose on the brain.

* have something on the brain 어떤 것을 계속 생각하다.

15. On second thought, She has made up her mind not to do it.

* make up one's mind 결정하다.

16. Finally telling the truth was a great weight off my shoulders.

* be a load / weight off one's shoulders / mind 부담을 덜다.

17. She opened her heart to me.

* open one's heart 마음을 열다.

18. We'll have to play it by ear.

* play it by ear 마음 내키는 대로 하다.

19. I couldn't believe my eyes when I first saw her.

* couldn't believe one's eyes 믿을 수가 없었다.

20. It must raise a few eyebrow.

* raise a few eyebrows 눈살을 찌푸리게 하다.

21. You should really discuss this with her face to face.

* face to face 서로 얼굴을 맞대고

22. I was pulling my hair out trying to squeeze an idea out of my brain.

* pull one's hair out 괴로워하다.

23. Don't lose your head.

* lose one's head 흥분하다.

24. If you have a bone to pick with me, just tell me what it is.

* have a bone to pick with ~에게 따질 일이 있다.

25. You have to stand on your own two feet.

* stand on one's own two feet 스스로 일어나다.

26. It'll take some time to find your own feet in a new job.

* find one's feet 자립하게 되다, 익숙하게 되다.

27. Keep your fingers crossed for me!

* keep one's fingers crossed 행운을 빌다.

28. I'm afraid I can't help you since I have my hands full.

* have one's hands full 매우 바쁘다.

29. We get our lines crossed.

* get one's lines / wires crossed 의도가 제대로 전달되지 않다.

30. I was happy to push the boat out for my son's success.

* push the boat out 홍청망청 돈을 쓰다, 잔치를 벌이다.

31. She was told to keep her mouth shut and not rock the boat.

* rock the boat 평지풍파를 일으키다.

32. If you don't buy now, you may find that you've missed the boat.

* miss the boat 기회를 놓치다.

33. Everybody is in the same boat.

* be in the same boat 똑같은 곤경에 처해있다.

34. His business has been in the doldrums for several years now.

* be in the doldrums 우울증에 빠지다, 그다지 성공적이지 못하다.

35. Your plans are anything but down-to-earth.

* down-to-earth 철저한, 현실적인, 실제적인

36. She's really stuck in a rut.

* be stuck in a rut 타성에 젖다.

37. I think they're middle-of-the-road and balanced.

* middle-of-the-road 중도의

38. She has an egg on her face.

* have egg on one's face 체면을 구기다.

39. My efforts will bear fruit.

* bear fruit 열매를 맺다.

40. I have to bite the bullet and back down on the demand.

* bite the bullet 고통을 참다.

Ⅲ. 문박사와 천박사의 일상영어회화

이 번장에서는 일상생활에서 유용하게 쓸 수 있는 표현을 알아보자. 먼저 각각의 표현을 Situation을 통해 적절히 파악한 후, Other Expressions를 통해 관련된 문장을 학습하도록 하자. 보다 자세한 사항은 문영수 · 천재윤(2005) 누워서 보는 영어를 참조하면 된다.

[Unit 1] She's cool.

각자 여러분이 생각하는 매력적인 이상형은 다르기 마련이다. 사람에게 cool을 사용하는 것은 '매력적이면서 사리분별이 뛰어나다'는 것이다.

Situation

A : What's her personality like? 그녀 성격이 어때?
B : She's cool. 그녀는 분별력이 있어.

Other Expressions 성격 I

01. He's withdrawn.
그는 내성적이다.

02. She's a dreamer.
그녀는 몽상가이다.

03. You're so sweet.
너는 매우 상냥해.

04. He's conservative.
그는 보수적이다.

05. It's no use turning on the charm.
매력을 발휘할 필요 없어.

06. There is no need to fly off the handle.
화를 낼 필요 없어.

07. She was panned by many people.
그녀는 혹평 받는다.

Vocabulary

- dreamer **몽상가**
- sweet **달콤한**
- conservative **보수적인**
- charm **매력**
- handle **손잡이, 도끼자루**

[Unit 2] What a nerve!

알다시피 nerve란 단어는 신경이란 뜻이다. 의미가 확장되어 위의 문장은 '뻔뻔스러운 녀석'이라는 뜻이 된다. 타인에 대해서는 비록 그 사람이 부족하고 미울지라도 좋게 평가하도록 노력해보자! 미처 발견하지 못한 그 사람의 장점이 어딘가에 분명히 있을 것이다.

Situation

A : I need your opinion. 저는 당신의 의견이 필요해요.
B : What a nerve! You hate me. 뻔뻔스럽군! 넌 날 미워하잖아.

Other Expressions 성격II

01. He doesn't take too much to set him off.
그는 다혈질이다.

02. She's got nerves of steel.
그녀는 강심장이다.

03. He's a down-to-earth kind of guy.
그는 현실적이다.

04. He's a negative.
그는 부정적이다.

05. She takes forever to make the simple matter.
그녀는 매우 우유부단하다.

06. She's difficult woman to approach.
그녀는 상대하기 힘든 여자다.

07. You can't do anything right.
너는 일을 제대로 하는 것이 없어.

08. She has a talent for making people feel comfortable.
그녀는 사람들을 편안하게 하는 재능을 가지고 있어.

Vocabulary

- nerve **신경**
- negative **부정적인**
- approach **접근하다**
- talent **재능**
- comfortable **편안한**

[Unit 3] What's the catch?

살아가면서 타인의 속마음을 파악하기란 하늘에 떠다니는 구름같이 걷잡을 수 없을 때가 많은 것 같다. 위 문장의 뜻은? '의도가 뭐야?' 정도로 파악하면 되겠다.

Situation

A : What's the catch? 의도가 뭐야?

B : Let's get to the point right now. 요점을 말하지요.

Other Expressions 의도

01. There's something I need to talk with you.
너에게 할 말이 있어.

02. Get to the point.
요점만 말해.

03. Don't hold anything back.
우물쭈물 하지마.

04. I know what you are thinking.
네가 무엇을 생각하는지 알아.

05. You look deep in thought.
너 생각에 몰두하고 있지.

06. I know better.
난 어리석지 않다.

07. That's a good point.
좋은 지적이다.

08. You trick me.
날 속이지마.

Vocabulary

- trick **속이다.**

[Unit 4] As I live and breathe.

우리는 흔히 자신의 결단을 말할 때 거부의 의사표현으로 '내 눈에 흙이 들어가기 전에는 어림도 없다'는 표현을 쓴다. 너무 극단에 치우치는 것보다 좀 더 합리적인 방법을 모색하는 것이 낫다.

Situation

A : Mom. I really want to marry her.
엄마, 그녀와 결혼할래요.

B : You can't marry her as I live and breathe.
내 눈에 흙이 들어가기 전에는 어림도 없다.

Other Expressions 결정

01. I've made up my mind.
결정했어.

02. I've already given this a lot of thought.
많이 생각해서 내린 결론이다.

03. That is what you have to do.
저것이 네가 해야 할 일이다.

04. There's nothing she can make me change my mind.
그녀가 어떤 말을 해도 내 마음을 바꿀 수 없어.

05. I've decided to immigrate to Korea.
나는 한국으로 이민가기로 했어.

06. This is my reason for existence.
이것이 내가 존재하는 이유다.

Vocabulary

- breathe 호흡하다
- make up one's mind 결심하다
- thought 생각
- immigrate 이민가다
- reason 이유
- existence 존재

[Unit 5] It's very G.

칭찬이 많은 사회는 멋진 사회이다. 서로에게 이렇게 말해보자. It's very G. G는 Great, Good의 축약형이다. 뜻은 '좋아, 멋지군요'이다.

Situation

A : I got a really nice job on my report card. 성적이 잘나왔어.
B : It's very G. 정말 잘했다. 멋져.

Other Expressions 칭찬

01. That's really good for a beginner.
처음치곤 잘합니다.

02. Nobody can touch you when it comes to that field.
그 분야에서 당신을 이길 수 있는 사람은 없어.

03. Nice job on your report.
보고서 잘했어.

04. That was very good for your first time.
초보자치고는 정말 잘했구나.

05. Is there anything you can't do?
네가 할 수 없는 것이 있니?

06. I'll try and improve next time.
노력해서 다음에는 더 잘할게요.

07. Thank you for noticing.
알아주셔서 감사합니다.

08. You must do better this time.
이번에는 잘해야 돼.

Vocabulary

- report card 성적표
- field 분야, 논, 밭
- improve 향상시키다 / improvement 향상
- notice 주목하다
- this time 이번에는

[Unit 6] I am working during the day and studying at night.

어렸을 때 풀숲에 반딧불이 참 많았다. 관련된 한자성어에 형설지공(螢雪之功)이란 말이 있다. 요즘처럼 과학이 발달한 시대에 형설지공이란 말이 구색하게 들릴지 모르겠지만 중요한 것은 열심히 한다는 것이다. 위의 표현은 '주경야독(晝耕夜讀)하고 있다'는 표현이다.

Situation

A : Don't be sleepy. 졸지 마렴.
B : Sorry, but I am tired. 죄송합니다. 피곤해서요.
I am working during the day and studying at night.
저는 낮에는 일하고 밤에 공부하거든요. 〈야간학교 상황〉

Other Expressions 학습

01. What's on the test?
무슨 시험이니?

02. The students has problems paying attention.
집중력에 문제 있어.

03. My teacher wanted to talk about my report.
선생님이 내 성적에 대해서 말씀하길 원하셨어.

04. Stop talking to your partner.
옆 사람과 이야기하지 마세요.

05. Raise your hand when I call your name.
호명하면 손드세요.

06. Let's get going.
시작합시다.

07. I need you to get into groups.
그룹으로 나누세요.

08. Please sit in your assigned seat.
지정석에 앉으세요.

09. Everybody should turn in your assignments at the end of class.
학기말까지 숙제를 제출하세요.

10. Can we turn it in by (an) e-mail?
이메일로 제출해 줄 수 있죠?

11. When is the test?
시험이 언제죠?

Vocabulary

- attention **주의**
- report **보고서, 성적표**
- assigned **지정된**
- assignment **숙제**

[Unit 7] Time to eat.

'밥 먹을 시간이야'라는 표현이다. 필자가 어렸을 때는 밥공기가 제법 컸다. 안에 담겨진 것보다 위로 올라온 것이 더 많았다. 요즘엔 청소년들 사이에 패스트푸드가 범람하고 있다. 외국에서는 주요 시간대에 패스트푸드 광고가 금지되고 있는 곳도 있다고 한다.

Situation

A : Time to eat. 밥 먹을 시간이다.

B : Would you set the table? 상 좀 차릴래?

Other Expressions 가정생활

01. When do you eat?
언제 먹죠?

02. Stop flipping channels.
채널 좀 바꾸지 마.

03. I overslept.
너무 잤다.

04. Can I take your coat?
옷을 받아드릴까요?

05. We better be going.

이제 가야겠어.

06. Would you like a taste?

맛 좀 보실래요?

07. Can you stay for dinner?

저녁까지 드시고 가세요.

08. We had a real nice time.

좋은 시간 보냈다.

Vocabulary

- oversleep 늦잠 자다
- flip 훌훌 넘기다

[Unit 8] Life isn't always what one likes.

'삶이란 뜻대로 되는 것은 아니다'라는 뜻이다. 하지만 더욱 노력해야겠죠? 그러면 언젠가는 그 꿈이 이루어질 것입니다. 명철한 판단과 노력만이 원하는 것을 성취하게 만든다.

Situation

A : I'll become a millionaire. 난 백만장자가 될 거야.

B : Life isn't always what one likes. 삶이란 뜻대로 되는 것은 아냐.

Other Expressions 의견I

01. I have a little different idea about that.
그것에 대해 다른 생각이 있어.

02. I don't agree with you on that point.
그 점에 대해 네 생각에 동의하지 않아.

03. Do whatever you want.
원하는 대로 해라.

04. What the hell are you talking about?
도대체 무슨 말을 하는 거야?

05. He has got it totally wrong.
그는 완전히 틀렸어.

06. What if this happen?
이 일이 발생하면 어쩌지?

07. I don't see it that way.
나는 그렇게 생각하지 않아.

08. You can say that again.
네 말이 옳다.

09. I'm afraid you've missed the point.
네가 요점을 놓쳤다.

Vocabulary

- millionaire **백만장자**
- whatever **무엇이든지**
- totally **전체적으로**
- miss **놓치다, 그리워하다**

[Unit 9] I'll circle on the calendar.

우리는 보통 중요한 약속이나 특정한 날을 표시하기 위해 달력에 공표를 해놓기 마련이다. 가끔 우리는 중요한 날을 잊어버려 곤란에 처하는 경우가 왕왕 있다. 위의 표현은 '중요한 날을 달력에 표시해 놓다'라는 표현이다.

Situation

A : I am wondering if you remember to go see a movie tomorrow.
내일 영화 보러가는 거 안 잊었지?

B : I really forgot. I'll circle on the calendar.
어, 깜빡했네. 달력에 표시에 놔야겠다.

Other Expression 약속

01. Are you still planning to get tonight?
오늘밤 약속 변동 없지?

02. Can't he take a rain check?
다음 기회로 미뤄도 될까요?

03. Let's push it back an hour to 7.
7시로 한 시간 미루자.

04. I'm getting tired of going there all the time.
항상 똑같은 장소에서 만나는 게 싫증나.

05. I have to cancel.
취소해야 될 것 같아요.

06. I won't be there.
나는 가지 않을 거야.

07. What's taking so long?
왜 이렇게 오래 걸리지?

08. She will be here on time.
그녀는 정시에 올 거야.

09. Did you call to see why she's not here yet?
그녀가 왜 안 오는지 전화했니?

10. Do you have her number?
그녀 전화번호 있니?

11. When will you get there?
언제 거기 갈 거야?

12. It won't happen again.
그 일은 다시 일어나지 않을 거야.

13. Do you think he forgot?
그가 잊었다고 생각하니?

Vocabulary

- wonder if ~인지 아닌지 궁금하게 여기다
- take a rain check 다음으로 미루다
- forget 잊다
- plan 계획하다. 계획
- cancel 취소하다

[Unit 10] Am I up?

모든 일에는 순서가 있기 마련이다. 이 우주의 끊임없는 생성과 사멸에는 일정한 원리가 존재하는 것이다. 질서를 거부할 때 인간은 많은 위험(?)을 자초하는 것이다. 위의 표현은 '이제 제 차례입니까?'의 뜻이다.

Situation

A : Next please. 다음

B : Am I up? 제 차례인가요?

Other Expressions 대기

01. When will I see you?
언제 보러 갈까요?

02. How much longer?
얼마나 걸리죠?

03. It'll be a few more minutes.
몇 분 더 걸릴 겁니다.

04. Is it OK to go on back?
돌아가도 될까요?

05. Are there many people ahead of you?
당신 앞에 많이 있나요?

06. She will be with you shortly.
곧 그녀가 너와 함께 할거야.

07. You can go in now.
지금 들어오세요.

08. Can you possibly make it any sooner?
곧 해주실 수 있죠?

09. Please wait here until the teller calls your number.
호명하실 때까지 여기에서 기다리세요.

10. Do you have any openings now?
빈자리가 있나요?

11. Do you have an appointment?
약속했나요?

12. We were here before.
전에 여기 왔지요.

13. Would you fill out this form?
이 양식 좀 작성해 주세요.

Vocabulary

- minute **분**
- shortly **바로, 곧**
- openings **빈 시간**
- ahead of **앞서**
- teller **수납직원**
- fill out **기입하다.**

[Unit 11] I'm so out of shape.

shape는 '몸매, 형태'라는 뜻이다. in은 안의 의미고 out of는 밖의 의미다. 따라서 의미는 '몸이 예전 같지 않다'라는 의미다. 건강만큼 일생을 살아가면서 중요한 것도 없는 것 같다.

Situation

A : I get worn-out too easily. 쉽게 피로합니다.
B : Me, too. I'm so out of shape. 저도요. 예전 같지 않아요.

Other Expressions 건강

01. What do you do stay in good shape?
건강유지로 무엇을 하죠?

02. I feel younger than ever.
예전보다 젊어진 것 같아.

03. I'm trying to flatten my stomach.
복부살을 빼기 위해 노력해요.

04. He works out regularly.
그는 규칙적으로 운동한다.

05. I've got to get back into working out again.
다시 운동을 시작해야 될 것 같아.

06. Do you get much exercise?
운동 많이 하니?

07. Why don't you go see a doctor?
병원에 가보는 게 어때?

08. My health is poor.
내 건강은 나빠.

09. I had a physical checkup last week.
지난주에 신체검사 했어.

Vocabulary

- worn-out **지친, 닳아빠진**
- shape **몸매, 형태**
- stay **머무르다, 유지하다**
- flatten **평평하게 하다.**
- regularly **규칙적으로**
- physical **신체의, 건강검진**
- checkup **검사**

[Unit 12] Money talks.

정신적 풍요로움을 느끼기엔 너무 물질문명이 발달하는 시대입니다. 위 표현은 '돈이면 다된다'라는 표현입니다. 돈이 말한다니 생각해 보자. 유전무죄. 슬픈 현실이다.

Situation

A : How can I do that? 어떻게 그것을 할 수 있죠?
B : Money talks. 돈이면 다돼.

Other Expressions 가격흥정

01. If I pay in cash, would you give me a better deal?
현금으로 결재하면 좀 낫나요?

02. If you buy more than one, I will give you a better one.
한 개 이상을 사면, 잘 해주실 수 있나요?

03. Could you come down a little?
좀 깎아주실 수 있나요?

04. How much can you pay?
얼마나 내실 수 있죠?

05. It's too much.
너무 비싸요.

06. That's a steal.

거저입니다.

07. I'm not making any money at that price.

그 가격에는 남지도 않아요.

08. All our prices are fixed.

정찰제입니다.

Vocabulary

- in cash **현금으로**
- deal **거래**
- steal **매우 저렴하게 산 물건, 훔치다.**
- fix **고정하다, 고치다.**

[Unit 13] Let sleeping dogs lie.

let은 '어떠한 상태로 두다, 시키다, 허락하다'의 의미다.
위의 표현은 '어떠한 문제를 확대시키지 말고 있는 그대로 두자'의 표현이다. 가끔은 있는 그대로가 좋을 때가 있다.

Situation

A : What should I do in this situation? 이 상황에서 어떻게 하죠?
B : Let sleeping dogs lie. 그냥 놔두세요.

Other Expressions 의견II

01. That's a good idea.
좋은 생각입니다.

02. Why don't you take a nap?
잠깐 낮잠 자는 게 어때요?

03. I think you should do it.
당신은 그것을 해야 합니다.

04. Go for it.
잘했어.

05. I need your opinion on something.
그것에 대해 네 의견이 필요해.

06. Any more bright idea?
좀 더 좋은 생각 있나요?

07. I don't think it will work.
그것이 효과가 있으리라 생각하지 않아요.

08. I feel that it should be against the law.
그것은 법에 반한 것이라 생각해요.

Vocabulary

- situation **상황**
- nap **낮잠**
- against the law **위법한**

[Unit 14] Can I tempt you?

술이란 많은 의미를 내포하고 있는 단어라 생각한다. 무엇보다도 기쁠 때나 슬플 때 함께 한다는 것이다. 'tempt'라는 단어는 '유혹하다'라는 뜻을 가지고 있다. 물론 문맥에 따라 다르겠지만 위의 표현은 '한 잔 할래?'의 의미다.

Situation

A : Can I tempt you? 한 잔 할래?
B : Good idea. How about a glass of beer? 좋아, 맥주 어때?

Other Expressions 술

01. How about one more drink?
한 잔 더 하실래요?

02. Let's down these beers and then go out.
이 맥주 마시고 나가자.

03. You're gonna have a hangover from hell.
숙취가 심할 겁니다.

04. He's a mean drinker.
그는 술주정이 심해.

05. I think I had a few too many.
나는 많이 마셨어.

06. My tolerance is less than it used to be.
주량이 예전보다 줄었어.

07. I'm a slow drinker.
나는 천천히 마셔.

08. It's not strong enough.
독하지 않아.

Vocabulary

- tempt **유혹하다**
- hangover **숙취**
- tolerance **관용, 주량**
- strong **술이 독한**

[Unit 15] The aftertaste is bitter.

'뒷맛이 쓰다'라는 표현이다. 한국식 표현과 같다고 생각하면 된다.

Situation

A : This restaurant is great for pizza. 이곳 피자맛이 좋아.
B : The aftertaste is bitter. 뒷맛이 쓴 것 같아.

Other Expressions 식사I

01. It's too sweet.
너무 달다.

02. There's no flavor.
맛이 없어.

03. Have you ever tasting anything more delicious?
더 맛있는 거 먹어본 적 있니?

04. The food melts in your mouth.
음식이 입에서 녹을 거야.

05. It needs something.
무언가가 빠졌어.

06. I'll explode.
배가 터질 것 같아.

07. I would never eat there.
거기에선 안 먹을 거야.

08. I've never been here before.
여기에 와본 적이 없어.

09. It's the worst place I've been to.
와본 중에 최악이다.

Vocabulary

- bitter **쓴**
- sweet **달콤한**
- flavor **맛, 향**
- melt **녹다**
- explode **폭발하다**

[Unit 16] We're just a phone call away.

away는 떨어짐을 나타내는 단어다. '어디에 있든지 전화 한 통화면 다 해결된다'는 의미이다. 위의 표현은 광고문구나 남자가 여자에게 데이트 신청할 때에도 쓰일 수 있는 표현이다.

Situation

A : Can you help me anytime? 언제든지 날 도울 수 있니?
B : OK. We're just a phone call away. 언제든지 전화주렴.

Other Expressions 전화

01. Women have a tendency to hog the phone.
전화를 오래 사용해.

02. She has an unlisted number.
전화번호가 등록되어 있지 않아.

03. May I ask what this is in regards to?
용건이 뭐죠?

04. May I ask what the nature of the call is about?
용건이 뭐죠?

05. Sorry for interrupting you.
방해해서 미안합니다.

06. I'm not sure if I have the right number.
맞게 전화했는지 모르겠군요.

07. How can I get hold of you?
기다리세요.

08. Did you change phone numbers?
전화번호 바꾸셨나요?

09. If you stay on the line, you will be automatically transferred.
좀 기다리시면 자동으로 연결됩니다.

10. The number is on my card.
이 번호는 카드에 있어.

11. I was told to call this number.
이 번호로 전화왔어.

12. You can get me during business hours at this number.
당신은 이 번호로 근무시간에 전화하실 수 있어요.

13. What number can I reach you?
번호가 어떻게 되죠?

Vocabulary

- anytime **언제든지**
- tendency **경향**
- unlisted number **전화번호부에 없는 번호**
- interrupt **방해하다**

[Unit 17] Fill it up.

주유소에서 '가득 채워주세요'하는 표현이다. 언어는 끊임없이 변화하고 있다. 즉, 예전에는 'Fill her up'이란 표현을 썼지만 차를 여성 명사로 받는다는 것은 현 상황에 맞지 않기 때문에 it을 사용하는 게 낫다.

Situation

A : Fill it up. 기름 좀 넣어라.
B : OK. We had better stop by at the next station.
그래. 다음 정거장에 잠깐 들르자.

Other Expression 차I

01. How often do you have to fill your car up?
얼마나 자주 기름을 넣죠?

02. How are you on gas?
기름은 어느 정도예요?

03. I'm running on empty.
기름이 바닥나 간다.

04. You need a ride.
태워다 드릴게요.

05. Going my ways.
내 길을 가다.

06. Kill the radio.
라디오를 꺼.

07. How do you pop the trunk?
트렁크 어떻게 열죠?

Vocabulary

- fill **채우다**
- empty **텅 빈**

[Unit 18] Hit the road.

여행은 바쁜 일상에서 벗어나 마음의 여유를 찾게 해준다. 여행지에서의 즐거움, 신선함 그리고 만남 등 모든 것이 기쁨을 준다. 위의 표현은 '떠나다, 출발하다'의 의미이다.

Situation

A : Hit the road. 떠나자.

B : Oh, we should stay longer as planned. 계획한 대로 좀 더 머무르자.

Other Expressions 출발과 도착

01. I wish I could go with you.
당신과 함께 했으면 해요.

02. Have a great trip.
멋진 여행 되세요.

03. What time will you be arriving?
몇 시에 도착할 예정이죠?

04. It's great to be back.
다시 와서 기쁘다.

05. Did you have a nice trip?
멋진 여행이었니?

06. You should call you when you come.
오면 전화해.

07. I can't wait until you get back.
네가 올 때까지 못기다려.

08. I'll miss you 당신을
그리워 할거야.

Vocabulary

- as planned **계획한대로**
- trip **여행**
- get back **돌아오다**
- miss **그리워하다, 놓치다**

[Unit 19] That's asking too much.

상대방에게 부탁을 하기 위해서는 상당한 예의가 필요하다. 어느 수준 이상의 부탁은 금하는 것이 좋을 것 같다. '그건 너무 지나친 부탁이다'라는 표현이다.

Situation

A : Could I borrow your car tonight? 오늘밤 차 좀 빌려줘.
B : That's asking too much. 그건 너무 지나친 부탁인데.

Other Expressions 부탁

01. Would you do me a favor?
부탁 좀 드려도 되나요?

02. Could you watch my bag?
제 가방 좀 봐 주시겠어요?

03. Could you give me a hand?
좀 도와 줄 수 있나요?

04. Would you mind watering it?
그것에 물 좀 뿌려 주셔도 되나요?

05. All you have to do is ask.
당신이 할 일은 부탁을 드리는 것입니다.

06. I need to ask you to do me a favor.
부탁 좀 드릴게요.

07. She turned me down.
그녀는 거절했어.

08. It depends.
하기 나름이다.

Vocabulary

- borrow **빌리다**
- favor **호의, 부탁**
- water **물을 주다**
- turn down **거절하다**
- depend **의존하다**

[Unit 20] Are you making progress?

모든 일이 자신의 뜻대로 되어 가면 좋겠지만 인생사가 그렇게 만만하지는 않다. '일이 진전되어 가나요?'의 표현이다.

Situation

A : Are you making progress? 일이 진전되어 가나요?
B : Yes, We made a killing with this model. 네, 아주 잘 되어갑니다.

Other Expressions 사업

01. We are losing market share this year.
올해 시장을 잃어가요.

02. You had better cut your expense.
비용을 줄이는 것이 좋겠다.

03. My company is in the red.
내 회사가 적자야.

04. I have a poor head for business.
사업이 적자다.

05. He is living from paycheck to paycheck.
그는 봉급으로 그럭저럭 살아간다.

06. Since I got a pay increase, things are looking up.
봉급이 올라서 좀 나아져 간다.

07. I am a little hard up this week.
이번 주는 좀 어렵다.

08. Money is no object.
돈은 문제가 아니다.

09. I must have the Midas touch.
돈버는 능력이 탁월한 것 같아.

Vocabulary

- share **몫**
- expense **비용**
- paycheck **봉급**
- increase **증가하다**

[Unit 21] I must be going now.

만남이 있으면 헤어짐이 있기 마련이다. 헤어짐과 만남, 만남과 헤어짐 모두 같은 선상에 있는 것이다. 위 표현은 '이제 가봐야겠다'의 의미이다.

Situation

A : I must be going now. 이제 가봐야겠다.

B : Thank you for visiting my house. 방문해줘서 고마워

Other Expressions 작별

01. Let's keep in touch.
연락하고 지내자.

02. Drop me a line anytime.
언제든지 소식 주세요.

03. I can't wait to see you again.
네가 보고 싶을 거야.

04. Please drop by the office again.
사무실에 잠깐 들러요.

05. Shall we meet again?
다시 만날까?

06. See you around.
잘 지내렴.

07. It's time you got going.
이제 떠날 시간이다.

08. I guess I'll see you tomorrow.
내일 만나기로 한 것 같아.

09. Is it OK to come by sometime?
언제든지 들려도 되죠?

Vocabulary

- keep in touch **연락하고 지내다**
- anytime **언제든지**
- office **사무실**

[Unit 22] My computer is frozen.

컴퓨터의 발달은 인간의 노동력을 엄청난 속도로 줄여주고 있다. 이러한 기기가 얼다니(?) 의미를 추측해 보자. '내 컴퓨터가 고장났다'의 의미이다.

Situation

A : Can I come to your home and use the computer?
당신 집에 가서 컴퓨터 좀 써도 될까요?

B : My computer is frozen.
컴퓨터가 고장 났는데요.

Other Expressions 컴퓨터

01. The printer is out of paper.
프린터에 종이가 떨어졌어.

02. I need you to print this content.
이것 좀 인쇄 해줄래.

03. What computer did you save it on?
어디에다 저장했니?

04. What are those filed under?
그 파일들 어디에 있지?

05. Are you sure you saved it under the file?
그 파일에다 저장한 것 맞니?

06. You must have saved it.
너는 틀림없이 저장했을 거야.

07. Something is wrong with this disk.
이 디스크에 문제가 있어.

08. Has it printed already?
벌써 인쇄했니?

Vocabulary

- freeze **얼다. 냉동시키다**
- content **내용**
- save **저장시키다**

[Unit 23] You've got to tighten your belt.

2012년 국 · 내외적으로 경기침체가 예상된다. 언젠가 신문에서 택시기사들이 연료를 아끼려고 대기 중에 있는 택시를 손으로 밀고 앞으로 나아간다는 기사를 읽었다. 그리고 웬만한 가전제품이나 의복을 수리해서 입는 사람도 많다고 한다. 위의 표현은 '허리띠를 졸라매야 합니다'의 뜻이다.

Situation

A : I am planning to fix that. 나는 고쳐서 쓸 거야.

B : You've got to tighten your belt. 허리띠를 졸라매야 해.

Other Expressions 수선

01. Can you repair this clothes?
이 옷 좀 수선해 주실 수 있나요?

02. Do your have leather laces?
가죽 끈이 있나요?

03. Can you put a patch over the knee?
무릎에다 헝겊을 덧대주실 수 있나요?

04. No sound is coming out.
소리가 나질 않아요.

05. I bought that computer a few weeks ago.
나는 몇 주 전 그 컴퓨터를 샀어.

06. It won't turn on.
전원이 들어오지 않아.

07. My stereo's gone haywire.
내 스테레오가 고장났어.

Vocabulary

- tighten **단단하게 하다 어렵게 하다**
- plan **계획하다**
- fix **고치다**
- leather **가죽**
- lace **끈**
- patch **헝겊 조각**
- haywire **건초를 동여매는 철사**

[Unit 24] I'm under a lot of pressure at work.

under는 어떠한 상태 아래에 있음을 표현한다. 예를 들면 공사 중이면 under construction이라 한다. 과도한 스트레스를 받는 직장인들을 보면 정말 안쓰럽다. 위 표현은 '일에 많이 시달립니다'의 뜻으로 쓰인다.

Situation

A : I'm under a lot of pressure at work. 정말 바빠.
B : I know, but you should finish the work. 끝내야만해.

Other Expression 업무

01. Let's try again after break.
잠깐 쉬었다 하자.

02. I'll take care of it right now.
내가 당장 처리할 것이다.

03. There's no time limit.
시간제한이 없어.

04. When do you need this?
언제 이것이 필요하니?

05. I'm working on it right away.
지금 하고 있습니다.

06. It's far from being completed.
일이 아직 끝나려면 멀었습니다.

07. I just got it done.
막 다 마쳤다.

08. How soon will you be done?
얼마나 빨리 마칠 수 있나요?

09. I'm just getting started.
이제 막 시작했어요.

Vocabulary

- pressure **압력**
- break **휴식**
- take care of **보살피다, 처리하다**
- time limit **시간제한**
- complete **완성하다**

[Unit 25] They are neck and neck.

스포츠 경기 중에 쓸 수 있는 표현으로 '그들은 막상막하(莫上莫下)다'라는 뜻이다.

Situation

A : He made a three-pointer. 그가 3점 슛을 넣었어요.
B : They are neck and neck. 막상막하네.

Other Expressions 관람

01. He won the game beating out the other man.
그는 상대자를 물리쳐 경기에 이겼어.

02. He uses every trick in this game, but he will fail.
그는 모든 속임수를 쓰지만 실패할 것이다.

03. She is an old hand at shooting guns.
그녀는 사격을 잘해.

04. My son likes watching sports instead of playing.
내 아들은 스포츠를 하는 것보다 보는 것을 좋아해.

05. I am an armchair athletic.
나는 스포츠 보는 것을 좋아해.

06. What time is the game on?
몇 시에 경기하지?

07. I don't understand the rules of this game.
나는 이 경기의 규칙을 모르겠어.

08. Scalping tickets is illegal.
암표는 불법이다.

09. It will be a good game.
좋은 경기가 될 거야.

Vocabulary

- neck and neck **막상막하**
- beat out **물리치다**
- every trick **모든 수단**
- old hand **숙련된 사람**
- instead of **~대신에**
- armchair **팔걸이의자**
- athletic **운동선수**
- illegal **불법적인**

[Unit 26] Everything checked out OK.

차가 필수품이 된지는 오래됐다. 하지만 몇 년을 기준으로 늘 새로운 모델이 나오니까 10년 이상 된 차는 왠지 구식의 느낌이 든다. 아무리 오래된 차라도 정기적으로 수리를 하면 타기에 괜찮을 것 같다. '이상이 없습니다'의 표현이다.

Situation

A : Everything checked out OK. 이상 없습니다.
B : I don' think so. It's leaking oil. 오일이 새는 것 같아요.

Other Expressions 차II

01. You can tell where there was a dent.
아직도 움푹 들어간 곳이 보입니다.

02. You overcharged me for labor.
인건비를 너무 많이 불렀다.

03. How much is all that going to cost?
얼마나 들죠?

04. How should I pay for an oil change?
오일 교환하는데 얼마예요?

05. He had better check it up.
그는 그것을 검사하는 것이 낫겠다.

06. It's using a lot more gas.
기름을 더 먹는 것 같아요.

07. The tires are getting old.
타이어가 노후화 되어간다.

08. You need to change the front right tire.
앞 오른쪽 타이어를 바꿀 필요가 있다.

Vocabulary

- leak **새다**
- dent **움푹 팬 곳**
- overcharge **부당한 값을 요구하다**

[Unit 27] You have to watch your weight.

요즘 언론에서 체중 빼는 프로그램이 상당한 인기를 얻고 있다. 그만큼 체중조절은 모든 이의 관심사항이다. 지나친 다이어트는 건강에 악영향을 끼치겠지만 적당하면 건강에 득이 될 것이다. 위의 표현은 '당신은 살찌는 것을 조심해야 해요'의 뜻이다.

Situation

A : You have to watch your weight. 살찌는 것을 조심해.
B : What do I need to do? 어떻게 해야지?

Other Expressions 검사

01. You'll feel better soon.
곧 나아질 거예요.

02. Is there anything I should avoid eating?
제가 피해야할 음식이 있나요?

03. It came back negative.
음성으로 나왔어요.

04. Can it be cured?
치료할 수 있을까요?

05. The child is playing sick.
아이가 아프다.

06. You need to come in for a follow-up next month.
다음 주에 재진하러 오셔야 합니다.

Vocabulary

- watch **조심하다**
- weight **무게**
- feel better **좋아지다**
- avoid **피하다**
- negative **음성의, 부정적인**

[Unit 28] I need a room for two.

'두 명이 묵을 방을 주세요'라는 표현이다. 여행이란 많은 것을 일깨워주는 것으로 삶에서 꼭 필요한 것이다. 정확한 여행관련 표현을 평소에 익혀 실전에 강해지도록 하자.

Situation

A : I need a room for two. 두 명이 묵을 방이 필요해요.
B : Come with me. 따라오세요.

Other Expressions 관광

01. When does the last bus come?
마지막 버스가 언제죠?

02. Where can I buy a bus pass?
어디서 버스패스를 사죠?

03. How much does the tour cost?
관광하는데 얼마죠?

04. I could show you around.
내가 구경시켜 줄께.

05. When does the show begin?
언제 쇼가 시작하지?

06. What is the admission fee?
입장료가 얼마죠?

07. I'd like to book a flight.
예약하고 싶습니다.

08. I need to leave early in the morning.
아침 일찍 떠날 거야.

09. Can I put my name on the waiting list?
대기자 명단에 넣어 줄 수 있나요?

10. I need to reschedule my flight.
다시 예약하고 싶어요.

11. When is the arrival time?
도착시간이 언제죠?

12. My luggage is missing.
짐이 분실됐다.

13. Can you get me a blanket?
담요 좀 주세요.

14. What's the price difference?
가격 차이가 얼마죠?

15. Do you have any vacancies?
빈자리가 있나요?

Vocabulary

- bus pass **버스패스**
- admission fee **입장료**
- flight **비행**
- waiting list **대기자 명단**
- reschedule **다시 계획하다**
- luggage **짐**
- blanket **담요**
- difference **차이**
- vacancy **빈방**

[Unit 29] I need a couple more minutes to decide.

음식점에서 메뉴를 선정하기는 그리 쉽지 않다. 어떤 라디오 프로그램에서 점심 메뉴를 추천하는 코너가 있는데 정말 다양한 제안이 나온다. 위의 표현은 '조금 있다가 시킬게요'의 뜻이다.

Situation

A : Would you like to order now? 지금 주문하시겠어요?
B : I need a couple more minutes to decide. 조금 있다가 시킬게요.

Other Expressions 음식주문

01. Everything looks good.
모두 맛있어 보여요.

02. I highly recommend it.
적극 추천합니다.

03. Make it a double on that.
두 개 주세요.

04. I'll try something new.
새로운 것 시킬래.

05. I am not ready to order.
결정 못했어.

06. I'll have this.
전 이걸로.

07. What do you recommend?
추천해 주세요.

08. There are too many choices.
종류가 너무 많아.

Vocabulary

- decide **결정하다**
- recommend **추천하다**
- order **주문하다**
- choice **선택**

[Unit 30] After you.

살아가면서 타인을 먼저 생각한다는 것이 그리 쉽지는 않다. 대부분의 사람들은 자신을 우선순위에 두기 때문이다. 위의 표현은 상대방에게 '먼저 내리세요, 타세요'의 의미로 쓰인다.

Situation

A : Are you getting off? 내리세요?
B : After you. 먼저 내리세요.

Other Expressions 교통

01. Is this seat taken?
자리 있나요?

02. I missed my stop.
지나쳤어요.

03. What's the fare?
요금이 얼마죠?

04. Which line goes downtown?
어떤 버스가 시내에 가죠?

05. This is where you get off.
여기서 내리세요.

06. I don't know if I'm on the right bus.
맞게 탔는지 모르겠어요.

07. Let me get off here.
여기서 내려주세요.

08. You got the wrong bus.
잘못 타셨어요.

Vocabulary

- get off **내리다**
- miss **놓치다. 그리워하다**
- fare **요금**

[Unit 31] What a sizzling day it is.

'날씨가 푹푹 찌는구나!'의 뜻이다. 개인마다 좋아하는 날씨는 다르다. 필자는 선선한 가을날을 매우 좋아한다. 그저 바라만 보고 있어도 청명한 가을 하늘은 머릿속까지 상쾌하게 해준다. 오늘 따라 어린시절 가을 운동회가 떠오른다.

Situation

A : I am sweating my butt off! 몸이 늘어진다.

B : What a sizzling day it is! 정말 푹푹 찌네!

Other Expressions 날씨

01. Where's that draft coming from?
어디서 바람이 들어오지?

02. Let's wait till the rain stops.
비가 그칠 때까지 기다리자.

03. Is it raining outside?
밖에 비가 오니?

04. What's the weather supposed to be like tomorrow?
내일 날씨는?

05. It looks like it's going to rain.
비가 올 것 같아요.

06. The weather is really unpredictable.
예측하기가 정말 어려워.

07. What's the temperature?
온도가 몇 도니?

08. My car is blanked with snow.
차가 눈으로 뒤덮였어.

Vocabulary

- sizzle **매우 덥다**
- draft **통풍, 외풍, 초안**
- be supposed to **예상되다**
- unpredictable **예측할 수 없는**
- temperature **온도**
- blank **뒤덮다**

[Unit 32] Talk about biting the hand that feeds you.

'배은망덕(背恩忘德)도 유분수(有分數)지'의 표현이다. 자신에게 음식을 주는 손을 물어 뜯다니! 세상을 살아가면서 감사의 마음을 전하고 살자.

Situation

A : He has dug his own grave. 그가 제 무덤을 팠어.
B : Talk about biting the hand that feeds him. 배은망덕도 유분수지.

Other Expressions 비난

01. You always say that.
그런 식으로 말하지 마.

02. It's so typical of him to say so.
그는 항상 그런 식으로 말해.

03. What a crazy thing to do.
그렇게 하다니.

04. You're so shortsighted.
근시안적이군요.

05. Stop putting me down.
윽박지르지 마.

06. Why did you stab me in the back?
왜 배반하지?

07. Oh, I like that!
(반어적으로)좋아!

Vocabulary

- grave **무덤**
- feed **먹이를 주다**
- typical **전형적인**
- shortsighted **근시안적인**
- stab **찌르다**
- back **등**

[Unit 33] He always puts up a good front.

옷은 날개라고 흔히 얘기한다. 깨끗하고 단정해 보이는 옷차림은 입은 사람에게는 자신감을 보는 사람에게는 즐거움을 준다. 위의 표현은 '그는 옷을 단정하게 입는다'라는 의미다.

Situation

A : Could you explain his fashion style to me?
그의 옷차림을 말해줄래?

B : He always puts up a good front.
그는 항상 단정하게 입어.

Other Expressions 옷 고르기

01. We don't carry pants in that size.
그 사이즈 바지는없어요.

02. Which style are you looking for?
어떤 스타일을 찾나요?

03. They aren't long enough.
바지가 좀 짧네요.

04. My size is a bit hard to find.
맞는 사이즈가 없네요.

05. It's too tight around the waist.
허리부분이 쪼여요.

06. This is nice.
이걸로 할래.

07. I don't see anything here that I want.
원하는 것이 없어요.

Vocabulary

- put up **어떤 태도를 밖으로 내보이다**
- look for **찾다**
- enough **충분한**
- tight **꽉 끼는**
- waist **허리**

[Unit 34] It is sink or swim.

과거 영국에서 마녀를 재판할 때 강물에 던지던 관습에서 유래되었다. '사느냐 죽느냐'의 뜻이다. 과연 누가 누구를 죽이고 죽임을 당한다는 것인가? 중요한 결정의 순간에 사용할 만한 표현이다.

Situation

A : I'll do my test. 나는 최선을 다할 거야.

B : It is sink or swim. 사느냐, 죽느냐의 문제야.

Other Expressions 죽음관련

01. You can't take it with you.
죽어서 가져가니.

02. All or nothing.
죽기 아니면 살기다.

03. The gang rubbed him out.
일당은 그를 죽였다.

04. He was lucky to get away with his life.
죽지 않은 것만 해도 다행이다.

05. You have my deepest sympathy.
조의를 표합니다.

06. It's a pity he died so young.

젊어서 죽다니.

07. I know how you feel.

당신 심정을 알아요.

08. I remember being with her.

그녀랑 함께 있었던 게 기억나.

Vocabulary

- sink **가라앉다**
- rub out **죽이다**
- lucky **운 좋은**
- sympathy **동정**
- remember **기억하다**

[Unit 35] He has got a screw loose.

두뇌의 기능이 정상적이지 못하고 나사가 풀린 것처럼 이상하게 보일 때 '그 사람 제정신이 아니야'의 의미로 쓰인다.

Situation

A : Everybody thinks he is eccentric. 사람들이 그가 이상하대.
B : Right. He has got a screw loose. 그는 제정신이 아니야.

Other Expressions 정신관련

01. I'll brain him when I get hold of him.
그를 잡으면 때려줄 거야.

02. I racked my brains all the morning.
아침 내내 생각해 봤어.

03. I've got to take a break to get my head together.
좀 쉬어야겠어.

04. She has rocks in his head.
그녀가 이상해.

05. Have you lost your marbles?
정신 나갔니?

06. I'm having suicide feelings.
자살충동이 느껴져요.

07. She has been having delusions.
그녀는 환청을 듣는다.

08. I'm really tense.
긴장이 돼요.

09. I can't control my temper.
화를 참을 수가 없어요.

Vocabulary

- eccentric **기이한, 괴짜인**
- screw **나사**
- loose **느슨한**
- rack one's brains **머리를 짜서 생각해 내다**
- suicide **자살**
- delusion **미혹, 기만, 망상**
- control **통제하다**
- temper **화, 기질**

[Unit 36] I don't feel up to par.

'몸이 별로 좋지 않다'는 표현이다. 건강에 많은 신경을 써야하는 시대이다. 물론 과거에도 그랬지만 현재는 더욱더 음식물부터 일반 환경까지 건강을 저해시키는 요소가 너무도 많다. 같은 뜻으로 'under the weather'를 이용한다는 것도 참고하자.

Situation

A : How are you feeling? 기분이 좀 어때?
B : I don't feel up to par. 별로 좋지 않아.

Other Expression 환자에 관한 것

01. When do you expect to be back up?
언제 회복할 것 같나요?

02. Another day's rest.
하루 더 쉬면.

03. I hope it's nothing serious.
심각한 것이 아니길 바래요.

04. Sorry I can't get up.
못 일어나서 죄송해요.

05. There were no complications.
합병증은 없었습니다.

06. What room is she staying in?
병실이 어디죠?

07. I appreciate you coming to visit.
병문안 와줘서 고맙다.

08. We should readmit her to the hospital.
그녀는 다시 입원해야 해.

Vocabulary

- up to par **건강한 좋은**
- expect **기대하다**
- back up **회복하다**
- complication **합병증**
- stay in **머무르다**
- appreciate **고맙게 여기다**
- readmit **다시 넣다, 재입원시키다**

[Unit 37] This is quite a layout.

우리가 말하는 가구나 장식품을 layout으로 표현하기도 한다. 즉, '집안 장식이 굉장하구나!'의 의미로 쓰이는 표현이다.

Situation

A : Do you like my home? 집 괜찮니?
B : This is quite a layout. 집안 장식이 굉장하구나.

Other Expressions 집안관련

01. It was disgrace to the family.
집안망신이다.

02. She seems to enjoy washing her dirty linen in public.
그녀는 집안망신 시키는 것을 즐기는 것 같아.

03. Who wears the pants around here?
누가 가장이야?

04. I'm tired of picking up after my kids.
아이들이 어질러 놓은 것을 치우는데 지쳤다.

05. The department store has wall to wall everything you need.
백화점에는 우리가 필요한 것이 다 있어.

06. You stay here and hold the fort.
집 좀 봐.

07. Temper runs in the family.
성질 급한 것은 유전이다.

Vocabulary

- layout 가구, 장식품
- disgrace 모욕
- in public 공공의
- fort 요새

[Unit 38] Do you have any opening?

요즘 취업하기가 하늘에 별 따기보다 어렵다고 한다. 어서 빨리 대한민국이 총체적 위기를 잘 극복하기 바라며 더불어 청년실업이 해결되기를 바라는 바이다. 위의 표현은 '빈자리 있나요?'라는 표현이다.

Situation

A : Do you have any opening? 빈자리 있나요?
B : Please submit your resume. 이력서를 보내주세요.

Other Expressions 일자리

01. I've been pounding the pavement for a week.
나는 일자리를 찾아 일주일 동안 돌아다녔다.

02. I am going to visit the employment agency for a job.
나는 일자리를 얻기 위해 직업소개소를 찾아갈 생각이다.

03. She's looking for a job opening.
그녀는 취직자리를 찾고 있어.

04. She wants to apply for your company.
그녀가 너의 회사를 지원하고 싶어 해.

05. I have finally landed a job.
직업을 구했다.

06. I'm calling to see if you have any opening.
빈자리가 있는지 전화드렸어요.

Vocabulary

- openings 공석
- submit 제출하다
- resume 이력서
- pound the pavement 거리를 돌아다니다
- employment agency 직업소개소
- apply for 지원하다

[Unit 39] It must have been an act of God.

'천재지변임에 틀림없다'란 뜻이다. 어린 시절 비가 많이 와서 하교길에 손에 손을 잡고 거리를 걷던 기억이 난다. 또 한 번은 눈이 무릎 위에까지 와서 밖에 나가지 못했던 적도 있다. 최근 일본의 대지진을 한 번 생각해 보자. 인간이 할 수 있는 것은 아무것도 없었다.

Situation

A : Heavy rain destroyed the village. 심한 비가 마을을 파괴했어.
B : It must have been an act of God. 천재지변임에 틀림없어.

Other Expressions 재난

01. This area is experiencing heavy snow.
이 지역은 폭설을 겪고 있다.

02. Heavy rain brought about overflow of the river.
폭우는 강의 범람을 일으켰어.

03. A major earthquake hit the territory at night.
대지진이 밤중에 그 지역을 강타했다.

04. Houses were burnt down one after another.
가옥이 차례로 불탔다.

05. They were crushed to death.
그들은 압사 당했다.

06. The plane crash took 177 lives.
비행기 사고는 177명의 목숨을 앗아갔다.

Vocabulary

- experience **경험하다**
- overflow **범람**
- earthquake **지진**
- territory **지역**
- one after another **차례로**
- crush **짓누르다**
- crash **충돌**

[Unit 40] The city is a hotbed for criminals.

갈수록 포악해지는 범죄사건을 보면 등골이 오싹해진다. 어디까지가 인간본성의 밑바닥인지 궁금해지지 않을 수 없다. '그 도시는 범죄자들의 온상이다'라는 표현이다.

Situation

A : Somebody ripped off my bike. 누군가 내 자전거를 훔쳐갔어.
B : The city is a hotbed for criminals. 그 도시는 범죄자들의 온상이야.

Other Expressions 범죄

01. They zeroed in on violent crime.
폭력범죄에 초점을 맞췄어.

02. There was a killing last night.
간밤에 한 명이 죽었어.

03. I am innocent of any wrongdoing.
나는 결백해.

04. The crime is committed every day.
범죄는 매일 일어난다.

05. He was convinced of drug smuggling.
그는 마약밀수 판결을 받았어.

06. He denies involvement in the murders.
그 살인에 연루된 것을 부인하고 있다.

07. He was fired because he had his hand in the till.
그는 돈을 착복해서 해고당했다.

08. She was murdered on her way back home.
그녀는 귀가 길에 살해당했다.

Vocabulary

- rip off **훔쳐내다**
- hotbed **온상**
- criminal **범죄자**
- violent **폭력적인**
- wrongdoing **잘못된 일**
- commit **저지르다**
- smuggling **마약 밀수**
- deny **부인하다**
- involvement **관련**
- murder **살인**
- till **돈 서랍**

[Unit 41] The enemy fell on our post last night.

인간은 자신의 목적을 위해서 타인을 죽이는 잔혹함을 가지고 있다. 2011년 한 해도 수많은 전쟁으로 많은 인명이 살상되었다. 위의 표현은 '적이 어젯밤에 우리 기지를 공격했다'라는 의미다.

Situation

A : The enemy fell on our post last night.
적이 어젯밤에 우리 기지를 공격했어.

B : Right. The enemy took us by surprise.
맞아, 적이 기습공격을 해왔어.

Other Expressions 전쟁

01. The bloodletting is a long way from over.
유혈사태가 끝나려면 시간이 걸린다.

02. Their faces smudged with night camouflage.
그들의 얼굴은 야간 위장 때문에 얼룩져 있어.

03. They made an assault on the fortress.
그들은 그 요새를 공격했어.

04. They are beefing up their own arsenals.
그들은 자국의 군비를 증강하고 있다.

Vocabulary

- enemy 적
- post 기지
- bloodletting 유혈
- smudge 오점, 얼룩, 더럽히다
- camouflage 위장, 위장하다
- assault 공격
- fortress 요새
- beef up 증강시키다
- arsenal 병기고, 군수품의 비축

[Unit 42] Society as a whole remains segregated.

인종차별은 꼭 없어져야 한다. 인간의 피부색이 인간의 본성보다 중요한 것은 아니다. 위의 표현은 '사회 전체적으로 인종차별이 남아있다'라는 표현이다. 아직까지도 현대사회의 인종차별은 인류를 하나로 화합시키는데 큰 저해요소로 남아있다.

Situation

A : The United States is a big melting pot.
미국은 인종의 도가니야.

B : Right, but society as whole remains segregated.
하지만 사회 전체적으로 인종차별이 남아있어.

Other Expressions 인종차별

01. They couldn't break through racial barriers.
그들은 인종차별을 극복하지 못했어.

02. She must be a red-neck.
그녀는 인종차별주의자일 거다.

03. He asked his people to put aside tribal rivalry.
그는 인종 간의 대립을 중지하도록 요청했다.

04. Apartheid is a political hot potato in that area.
인종차별 정책은 그 지역에서 심한 논쟁거리야.

Vocabulary

- society **사회**
- remain **남아 있다.**
- segregated **분리된, 인종차별을 하는**
- put aside **중지하다**
- tribal rivalry **인종 간 대립**
- apartheid **인종차별**

[Unit 43] We turned thumbs up on his proposal.

의견이 다르다고 남과 내가 적이 될 수 없고, 상대방의 의견을 무시할 수도 없다. 또한 소수의 의견이 옳을 수도 다수의 의견이 틀릴 수 도 있다. '우리는 그의 의견에 동의했다'라는 표현이다.

Situation

A : We turned thumbs up on his proposal.
우리는 그의 의견에 동의했어.

B : It was a good deal.
잘했어.

Other Expressions 찬성, 동의

01. We are all for his suggestions.
우리는 그의 의견에 동의한다.

02. That's all that matters.
그게 중요해.

03. I gave the green light to the project.
나는 계획을 허가해 주었어.

04. I couldn't agree with you more.
네 의견에 전적으로 동감이야.

05. They share the view.

그들은 공통된 의견을 가지고 있어.

Vocabulary

- thumb 엄지
- proposal 제안
- deal 거래
- suggestion 의견, 제안
- green light 찬성
- share 나누다
- view 견해, 의견

[Unit 44] Play it cool.

살면서 일을 그르치지 않으려면 항상 여유를 가지고 행동하는 것이 중요하다. 물론 자신이 처한 상황이 극한이라면 그러한 여유를 찾는 것이 쉽지는 않다. '여유를 가져라'라는 표현이다.

Situation

A : I'll get time to catch my breath. 나는 잠깐 쉴 시간을 가질 거야.

B : Play it cool. 여유를 가지고 해.

Other Expressions 여유, 여가

01. You had better slow down.
여유를 가져.

02. You had better let up on that project.
그 계획을 늦추는 것이 좋겠다.

03. He gives his free time to golf.
그는 여가에 골프를 친다.

04. I raised my spirit by listening to music.
나는 음악을 들으면서 기분전환을 해.

05. I'll be able to see the light of day.
나는 한가해질 수 있을 것이다.

Vocabulary

- slow down 늦추다
- project 계획
- raise one's spirit 기분전환을 하다
- be able to ~할 수 있다

[Unit 45] Just stand your ground.

옳다고 생각하는 일에 자신의 신조를 지킬 줄 아는 세상이 되어야 한다. 이익에 따라 적과 아군을 구분하는 것은 잘못된 일일까? 독자 모두 생각해 보자. '당신의 입장을 고수해라'의 의미다.

Situation

A : Just stand your ground. 당신의 입장을 고수해.

B : I will continue to carry a torch. 끝가지 흔들리지 않을 거야.

Other Expressions 고수, 고집

01. I'll stick to my guns on this matter.
이 문제에 관해서는 내 입장을 고수할 거야.

02. She'll carry her point after all.
그녀는 자기주장을 관철시킬 거야.

03. He persisted in his opinion.
그는 자기주장을 고집했다.

04. I came on strong at the meeting.
나는 회의에서 강하게 주장을 펼쳤어.

05. He has a strong personality.
그는 성격이 강해.

Vocabulary

- stand one's ground 고수하다
- carry one's point 관철시키다
- persist in 주장하다
- personality 인격

[Unit 46] I'd better do some homework before I start.

어떤 일이든 시작하기 전에 사전 준비가 필요하다. 왜냐하면 준비 없이 의욕만 가지고 일을 시작하면 실패할 확률이 높기 때문이다. 위의 표현은 '시작하기 전에 사전준비를 해야겠다.'라는 표현이다.

Situation

A : I'd better do some homework before I start.
시작하기 전에 사전 준비를 해야겠어.

B : That's a good idea.
좋은 생각이야.

Other Expressions 준비

01. We must provide against (for) the accident.
우리는 그 사고에 대비해야 한다.

02. Take your coat just in case.
만일의 경우에 대비하여 코트를 가져가.

03. I am all set to buy it.
나는 그것을 살 준비가 다 되어 있어.

04. He just came in cold.
그는 아무런 준비 없이 왔어.

05. I rolled up my sleeves.
나는 본격적으로 일할 채비를 다했어.

Vocabulary

- had better **~하는 것이 낫다**
- just in case **만일의 경우에**
- came in cold **준비 없이 오다**
- roll up one's sleeves **본격적으로 준비하다**

[Unit 47] He seems to be in the hot seat right now.

인생은 누구에게나 힘든 시기가 꼭 온다. 그러나 그러한 역경을 딛고 일어서는 것이 인생의 과정이 아닐까 싶다. 매사에 포기하지 말자. 위의 표현은 '그는 지금 어려운 처지에 있는 것 같다'라는 의미다.

Situation

A : He seems to be in the hot seat right now.
그는 지금 매우 어려운 처지에 있는 것 같아.

B : He is really in the doghouse.
그는 정말로 궁지에 몰렸어.

Other Expressions 곤경, 궁지

01. I am a jam now because my car has broke down.
차가 고장이 나서 우리는 지금 곤란한 상황에 있다.

02. I'm in a fix because I lost my wallet.
지갑을 잃어버려서 곤란한 상황이다.

03. I didn't know you were hard up against it.
나는 네가 곤경에 빠져 있었다는 것을 몰랐다.

04. I felt like a fish out of water in the party.

나는 파티에서 어색했다.

05. Am I embarrassing you?
저 때문에 난처합니까?

Vocabulary

- break down **고장 나다**
- be in a fix **곤란한 상황에 있다**
- wallet **지갑**
- embarrass **당황하게 하다**

[Unit 48] He was a big hit.

'그는 대성공했다'라는 의미다. 성공의 기준을 어디다 두냐에 따라 성공의 의미가 다르겠지만 말이다. 언젠가는 필자도 독자 여러분도 세상적 기준으로 큰 성공을 거둘 것이다.

Situation

A : He rose in the world. 그는 대성공했어.

B : Right, he was a big hit. 맞아. 대성공이었어.

Other Expressions 성공

01. He tries to gain face.
그는 권세를 얻으려고 애써.

02. Such a person is bound to get on in life.
그런 사람은 반드시 성공한다.

03. I'm sure he will make out in that job.
나는 그가 성공할거라고 확신한다.

04. She made her way in the world with dance.
그녀는 춤으로 성공했다.

05. Don't worry. You can pull it off.
걱정하지 마, 너는 잘 할 수 있어.

06. He made his own way in the world.
그는 자수성가했다.

Vocabulary

- gain **얻다**
- make out **성공하다**

[Unit 49] Do it at the peril of your life.

'목숨을 걸고 해라'의 의미다. 요즘은 경쟁이 심해서 목숨을 걸지 않고(?) 성공하는 일은 거의 없다고 봐도 과언이 아니다. 쉽사리 무엇인가를 이루려는 생각은 버려야 한다. 노력! 노력! 또 노력!

Situation

A : I'll try and do it one way or another. 어떻게든 해 보겠다.

B : Do it at the peril of your life. 목숨을 걸고 해라.

Other Expressions 모험, 위기

01. They were in peril of death from hunger.
그들은 굶어죽을 위기에 처해 있다.

02. He was up a tree.
그는 더 이상 도망갈 데가 없었다.

03. I think that democracy is in crisis.
나는 민주주의가 위기에 처해 있다고 생각해.

04. I risk my neck out to do something for my baby.
아기를 위해 목숨을 걸었어.

05. My prestige and honor are on the line.
내 위신과 명예가 위기에 놓여있어.

Vocabulary

- peril 위험
- death 죽음
- democracy 민주주의
- prestige 위신
- honor 명예

[Unit 50] She eats like a bird.

식사를 매우 조금 하는 사람을 일컫는다. 필자 주위에도 식사뿐만 아니라 모양새도 새처럼 먹는 사람이 있다. 잘 먹어야 건강하고 활기차게 하루를 보낼 수 있다. '그녀는 새처럼 먹는다'라는 의미다.

Situation

A : She eats like a bird. 그녀는 새처럼 먹어.

B : Really? I can't believe it. 정말이야? 믿을 수가 없군.

Other Expressions 식사II

01. She is on a diet.
그녀는 다이어트 중이야

02. I am a vegetarian.
나는 채식주의자다.

03. He always eats like a pig.
그는 돼지처럼 먹어.

04. The mere smell put me off the food.
냄새만으로 식욕이 없어졌어.

05. He had bigger eyes than his stomach.
그는 과식했어.

06. It really turns me off.
정말로 나를 역겹게 한다.

07. I've scratched the surface.
이제 막 먹기 시작했어.

Vocabulary

- be on a diet **다이어트를 하다**
- vegetarian **채식주의자**
- smell **냄새를 맡다**
- stomach **위**
- surface **표면**

Ⅳ. 문박사와 천박사의 관광영어회화

이 번 장에서는 출국에서 입국까지 관광영어회화의 전반적인 흐름에 대해 알아보자. 문박사와 천박사의 관광영어회화를 통해 외국인과의 대화에 자신감을 가져보도록 한다. 더불어 보다 세밀한 관광영어회화 학습을 원하는 독자는 문영수 · 천재윤(2011) Survival Tourism English를 참조하기 바란다.

Section 1 Airline Service

Chapter 1 Check-In Service

Reservation

A : Asiana Airlines. How may I help you, sir?

P : I have an open ticket for Chicago and I'd like to make a reservation for a flight to Chicago.

A : When would you like the reservation for?

P : By flight next Sunday.

A : Right. Hold on, please...., we have two flights at 9 a.m. and 4 p.m., what time would you like to make it?

P : At 4 p.m.

A : What class would you like?

P : Economy, please.

A : All right. Your name and cell phone number, please?

P : My name is Young-soo Moon and 010-4654-9718.

A : O.K. Your reservation is made for(= is booked for) flight 320 to Chicago next Sunday at 4 p.m.
You can call me, if there is any change in the flight time.

P : That's all right. Thank you very much.

A : Don't forget your flight time.

*A : Airline agent   P : Passenger
*Will you be flying one-way or round-trip?
*When would you like to return?
*Let me check if seats are available?
*Please be sure to check-in at the airport one hour before your flight is scheduled to leave.

Reconfirmation

P : Hello. This is Young-soo Moon. I'd like to reconfirm my reservation.

A : What reservation are you holding?

P : I've made a reservation for your flight 320 leaving tomorrow at 4 p.m. to Chicago.

A : How many are there in your party, sir?

P : Just one.

A : Hold on, please...., you're booked on our flight 320 to Chicago tomorrow.

*Your name and flight number, please?
*Just a moment, please.

Changing and Cancelling Schedule

A : Japan Airlines. May I help you sir?

P : Could you change my flight time for tonight at 9 o'clock to tomorrow at 4 p.m.
(I'd like to cancel my reservation for tonight.)

* I'd like to change flights.
* Your reservation is cancelled.
* Anything else I can do for you today, sir?
* Passengers can now be ticketed electronically.

Ticketing

A : Good morning. May I help you, sir?

P : I'd like to purchase my ticket. I already have a reservation. My reservation number is AA 200.

A : Your name, please?

P : Young-soo Moon

A : Yes, sir. 2 p.m. Saturday, Asiana Airlines, right?

P : Right. How much is the fare?

A : It's $ 990 for round-trip.

P : Do you accept BC card?

A : Sure. May I have, please?

P : Here you are.

....

A : Would you like to sign here, please?

P : O.K.

A : Here is your ticket for Chicago, economy class, on Flight 005 leaving at 2 p.m. on October 14th.

Check-In

P : Is this right counter to check in for this flight?

A : Yes, it is. May I have your passport and ticket, please?

P : Here you are.

A : How many pieces of baggage do you have?

P : Two. I'd like a window seat.

A : Right, please put your baggage on this scale.

P : O.K. Is the plane on schedule?

A : Yes, it is. Please be present at the boarding gate 20 minutes before departure time.

* 탑승수속(Check-In)은 출국의 첫 번째 단계로서 승객이 좌석을 배정 받고 수하물을 부친 후 탑승권을 받는 과정이다. 출국시 절차는 1. 탑승수속(Boarding procedures) 2. 출국 일반 대합실(Departure waiting Area) 3. 보안 검색(Security check) 4. 휴대물 검사(Carry-on check) 5. 출국심사(Emigration check) 등이다.

Request of boarding station

P : Excuse me. I want to board OZ Flight 320 to Chicago. But is this the way to Gate 5?

C : Oh, it's. Go straight on and turn left. You'll see a sign.

P : Thank you very much.

C : You hurry-up, please!

* P : Passenger C : Crew
* boarding card = boarding pass 탑승권
* boarding list 탑승 승객 명부

Chapter 2 Check-In Announcements

1. Announcement in the airport

Flight OZ 411 to Los Angeles due to depart at 10:00 is now boarding at Gate 8.

2. Government formalities for departure

May I have your attention, please? Passengers who have not finished the formalities for departure are requested to come to the customs office immediately.

3. Check-in

May I have your attention, please? Passengers for Asiana Airlines Flight OZ 411 bound for Los Angeles departing at 10:30, please go through check-in and baggage check at Asiana check-in counter. Thank you.

4. Security check-in

May I have your attention, please? Passengers for Korean Airline Flight KE 500 bound for Chicago at 12:30, please have your travel card and passport ready and proceed to the departure lounge. Thank you.

5. Departure delayed

Your attention, please. Asiana Airlines announces the departure of Flight No. 320 for Chicago at 4 p.m. This Flight 320 bound for Chicago is now in its final boarding. Please proceed to the boarding gate.

....................Asiana Airlines announces Flight No. 320 has been behind schedule

* Further information will be announced as soon as possible, thank you.

6. Boarding

Your attention, please. Asiana Airlines announces the departure of Flight OZ 411 for Los Angeles. Those with first-class tickets, small children, or needing assistance please board at this time. Our staff is ready to assist you. We will cal for other passengers in a few minutes. Thank you for flying Asiana Airlines today.

Economy class passengers holding boarding cards with seat numbers between rows 35 and 50 are requested to board now.

Chapter 3 Before Take-off Service English

At the boarding station

S : May I help you find your seat?

P : Yes, please. Where is 27-H?

S : This way, please. Your seat is right over there by the window.

P : Thank you.

S : Would you show me your boarding pass, please?

T : Here you are.

S : It is right over there on the aisle.

T : By the way. I'd like a window seat. May I change my seat.

S : That's not the case.

* That's not the case 그럴 수 없어요. 그러한 경우가 없어요.
** S : Stewardess P : Passenger T : Traveler

Announcements

Good afternoon. Ladies and gentlemen. We wish to welcome you aboard this flight ....

Please be certain your seatbelt is fastened and abstain from smoking until the No Smoking sign is turned off. Please press the call button if you need any help. Thanks.

Boarding-Conversation

P : A lovely day, Right?

T : It certainly is.

P : Excuse me, but could I have your name please?

T : It's John, John Smith.

P : Mr. Smith. My name is Young-soo Moon. I'm Korean. Nice to meet you. Are you British?

T : No. I'm American. Excuse me, what do you do for a living?

P : Professor and pastor.

T : Oh, Is that so? what is your purpose of going to Chicago?

P : To visit Moody Church and travel the country.

T : Well, nice to have met you. Hope you'll enjoy your stay in Chicago.

Seating arrangements

P : May I sit here?

T : I'm afraid this seat is taken.

P : Oh, is it?

T : Yes, Why don't you ask the stewardess when she comes by? She should be able to help you find one.

....

P : I'd like to change my seat.

S : All Right. This way, please. We have lots of vacant seats at the window. I'm sure
you'll be delighted with it.

P : Thank you.

*I'm sorry, but I'm afraid you're in the wrong seat.
*I'll see if it can be arranged.
*I'll check it for you immediately.
*Excuse me, may I change my seat?
*We have lots of empty seats at the back.
*Could you tell me where my seat is?

Beverage service

S : Hello. What would you like to drink? We have orange juice, coffee and wine.

P : Orange juice, please.

T : Excuse me, may I have something to drink?

S : Sure. What would you like?

T : What do you have?

S : We have complimentary coffee and alcoholic beverages. Here's a beverage list for other drinks.

T : I'd like to have a glass of whisky, please.

* complimentary coffee 기내에서 서비스로 제공하는 커피
* Can I have another drink?
* My drink is too strong.
* Would you care for a refill?

Meal service

S : Which would you prefer, steak or spiny lobster?

P : Spiny lobster, please.

....

S : Do you have finished your dinner, sir?

P : Yes, I enjoyed it very much.

S : What would you like for dessert, sir? We have a choice of ice-cream or cake.

P : No, thank you. You see. I'm on a diet.

S : You'd like a cup of coffee or orange juice instead.

P : Coffee, please.

* May I take your meal tray, sir?
* No, I'm not finished, yet.
* I'm sorry sir, please take your time and enjoy your meal.
* Will you be serving meals, soon.

Newspaper service

S : Would you like a paper?

P : Yes, please.

T : May I have a magazine or something?

S : Certainly. Just a moment. I'll be right back with one. Which do you prefer, one in Korean or English?

T : One in English, please.

S : All right, sir.

* paper 신문(newspaper)

Blanket service

P : Excuse me. Could I have a blanket?

S : I'm afraid there aren't any at the moment. Can you wait just a little while?

P : O.K. I will.

S : I'll bring you one as soon as I find one available.

P : Would you, please? Thank you.

T : I'd like to have a nap. May I have one more blanket, please?

S : I'm sorry. Can you wait just a little while?

Sick passenger

S : You look kind of pale. What's the matter?

P : I feel like vomiting.

S : Do you? Just a minute. Let me get the airsick bag ready.

....

Here.

P : Thank you. Excuse me, do you have any medicine for a digestive?

S : All right, sir.

*vomit 토하다(throw out)
*Here is an airsick bag for you.
*Just in case you vomit, sir.
*Is there anything I can do for you, sir?
*I hope you feel better.
*How are you feeling now, sir?
*Can I get you anything else?
*I'm sorry, but we don't have anything for a sore throat.

Facilities service

P : Excuse me. How do I adjust the ventilation?

C : Please turn the knob, sir.

P : And how do I adjust the volume?

C : Just turn this dial, sir. Do you know how to change channels?

P : I have no idea

C : Just turn this dial, sir.

P : Will you show me how I turn on and off the light?

C : Please push the switch that looks like a light bulb.

P : Where can I plug in the earphone?

C : Right here, sir.

P : I'm very sorry, but I have one more question. How do I recline my seat and return it to the upright position?

C : Just push this button, lean back and lean forward.

P : Thank you very much.

* P : Passenger   C : Cabin crew

In-flight shopping 1

C : May I help you?

P : I'd like to buy neckties. Do you have Giantone Tie?

C : Yes, we have. How about this one?

P : I like it. How much do I owe you?

C : Twenty-five dollars, sir.

P : Can I pay by charge?

C : Of course.

* charge 신용카드(credit card)
* Can I pay in Korean won?
* How much is it in won?
* May I take your order for any duty free items, sir?
* What do you have?
* The shopping guide will tell you.

In-flight shopping 2

P : Would you show me some cosmetic, please?

C : Right. What brand do you want?

P : I want to buy some Christian Dior.

C : Hello. What are you looking for?

T : I want to buy some cigarettes. What kind of cigarettes do you have?

C : We have Glory, Marboro, Sallem.....and so on.

T : I want Glory. Five packs, please.

Transit passenger announcement

Your attention, please. We shall be arriving in Anchorage after three minutes. Please make sure that seat belts are fastened, and extinguish all cigarettes. This plane will stay to Anchorage Airport an hour.

Transit passenger

T : I'm changing flight. Are you changing flight, too?

P : No, I am not.

S : Are you a transit passenger?

P : Yes.

S : Please receive transit card. Don't you leave anything valuable!

P : Right. What's the boarding time?

S : At 6:20 p.m.

Your attention, please. Transit passengers, Please wait at the lounge. The gate number for Northwest .... Airlines to Chicago is 10.

* transit passenger 통과여객 혹은 경유 손님(주유나 기타 사정에 의해 경유지에서 기내 밖으로 나와 잠깐 쉬는 여행객)

Changing flight

S : Are you a transit passenger, sir?

T : No. I'm changing flight.

S : What is your connecting flight?

T : I have to take a connecting flight to Atlanta. Where can I confirm my flight?

S : Go to the Airlines desk, please.

Chapter 5 Check-out Service English

Immigration 1

I : Hello. You passport, please?

P : Here it is.

I : What's the purpose of your visit?

P : To travel the country.

I : How long are you staying in America?

P : For two weeks.

I : O.K. Go ahead and find your baggage, please.

P : Thank you.

* May I see your passport, sir?
* How long are you going to stay?
* How long do you intend to stay?
* You may go to customs now.

Immigration 2

I : Hello. What's the purpose of your trip?

P : For Sightseeing.

I : How long will you be in the United states?

P : For two weeks.

I : Enjoy your trip.

P : Thank you.

I : Next, please. May I see your passport?

T : Here you are.

I : I see you are on a business visa. How many are there in your party?

T : Just one.

Baggage claim

P : Excuse me, but where is the baggage claim area?

W : Over there. Do you have your baggage check?

P : Yes, I have.

P : I can't find baggage. Will you please?

W : I'll try to find them.

P : Thank you.

*Where can I pick up luggage from Asiana Flight?
*Will you please help me to find them?
*Could I see your baggage claim tag?
*We're very sorry about your inconvenience.

Customs

C : Hello. Do you have your customs declaration form, please?

P : Here it is.

C : Are these all your bags?

P : Yes, they are. Here is my passport.

C : Thank you. Do you have anything to declare?

P : No, I don't. I only have personal effects.

C : Do you have any gifts, or valuable articles?

P : No, I don't.

C : Do you have more than five thousand dollars?

P : No.

C : Then, go through the green channel.

P : I see. Thank you.

* 입국시 절차는 1. 입국 심사 2. 보안 검색 3. 수하물 회수 4. 세관 검사 5. 입국 일반 대합실 등이다.

* May I see your customs declaration form, please?

Chapter 6 Preparation for return

Reconfirmation

P : Hello. This is Young-soo Moon. I'd like to reconfirm my reservation.

A : What reservation are you holding?

P : I've made a reservation for your flight 156 leaving tomorrow at 2 p.m to Seoul.

A : How many are there in your party, sir?

P : Just one.

A : Hold on, please..., you're booked on our flight 156 to Seoul tomorrow.

* P : passenger A : Airline agent

Seeing off

A : Here we are at the airport.

P : It's very nice of you to see me off.

A : My pleasure. I hope you have a nice trip.

P : I am very grateful to you for your kind hospitality during my stay here. I'd better go and check in at the counter. Good-bye.

Checking-In

A : May I have your passport and ticket, please?

P : Here you are.

A : How many pieces of baggage do you have?

P : Two. I'd like a window seat.

A : Right, please put your baggage on this scale.

Boarding station

P : Excuse me. I want to board OZ Flight 156 to Seoul. But is this the way to Gate 7?

A : Oh, it's. Go straight on and turn left.

P : Thank you very much.

Announcement

Your attention, please. Asiana Airlines announces the departure of Flight No. 156 for Seoul at 2 p.m. This Flight 156 bound for Seoul is now in its final boarding. Please proceed to the boarding gate.

Section 2 Hotel Service

Chapter 1 Check-In Service

B : May I help you with your baggage?

P : Please. Where can I register?

B : Come this way, please.

* B : Bellman P : Passenger
* I'm sorry sir, we're fully booked.
* Here is your key card.
* If you need anything, please call us.
* I have a reservation.
* Just a moment. I'll check the list.
* We have your reservation.

Front Desk 1

P : Hello. I'd like to check in. My name is Jae-Yun Cheon and I have a reservation for a single room with bath.

C : Oh, yes. Mr. Cheon. We have your reservation. Would you fill out this registration form, please?

P : O.K. Will this do?

C : Fine. You are in room 1517. Here is your key. I'll call a bellman to carry up your baggage.

* C : Clerk
* I'll have the bellman help you with your baggage.
* How long are you going to stay?
* What kind of room do you have in mind, sir?

Bellman

B : Are these all your bags?

P : Yes, they are.

B : Right this way. Well, here we are. This is your room.

P : It's very nice room.

B : If you need more assistance, call me.

P : O.K. Thank you for your help.

B : You're welcome. Enjoy your stay.

Front Desk 2

P : Excuse me, but where is the reception desk?

D : At the front desk over there to your left, sir.

....

C : Good evening. Do you have a reservation?

P : Sure. I made a reservation in Seoul. My name is Jae-Yun Cheon.

C : Right. Will you fill in this registration form, please?

P : Here you are.

C : Fine. You are in room 1112. Here is your key.

P : O.K. Thank you for your help,

Reservation 1

R : Hilton Hotel. May I help you?

P : Hello. I don't have a hotel reservation and just arrived at the airport. I want to reserve a double room with bath for this evening. Do you have?

R : Yes, we have.

P : What's the room rate?

R : Thirty dollars a night including tax.

P : O.K. I'll take room. My name is Jae-Yun, Cheon. At the hotel by six o'clock.

* R : Reservationist
* What's your rate per night?
* I want a quiet room with a good view.

Reservation 2

P : Good morning. I arrived without reservation a hotel. Do you have a twin room for tonight?

R : Are you going to stay here just for tonight?

P : Yes.

R : I'm sorry. We are full tonight.

P : Can you suggest another hotel?

Reservation 3

P : Hello. This is Jae-Yun, Cheon. I'd like to confirm my

reservation.

R : What reservation are you holding?

P : I've reserved a double room for three nights.

R : Hold on, please...., We have your reservation.

Without Reservation 1

P : Can I have a room, please?

W : Yes, we have a nice room on the third floor.

P : How much is it?

W : Twenty dollars per night, plus tax and service charge.

P : May I see the room?

W : Sure. Come this way, please.

P : Take this room, please.

Without Reservation 2

P : Hello. I want a room, please.

W : What kind of room would you like?

P : I'd like a twin room with a nice view.

W : All right. sir. We have one good room vacant on the second floor. How long will you be staying here?

P : Three nights.

W : Right this way. Well, here we are. This is your room.

P : It's very nice room.

W : If you need more assistance. call me.

Without Reservation 3

P : Do you have a double room?

W : Yes, How long will you be staying here?

P : Two nights. What is the room rate?

W : Twenty-five dollars per night.

P : Does it include the tax and service charge?

W : Sure.

P : How much is it?

W : About fifteen percent.

Check-In : Expressions

Do you have a room available?

How much does the room cost?

A cheap and clean room, please.

Is breakfast included in the charge?

Will you please have my baggage taken up to my room?

Where is the security box?

Where is the closet for my clothes?

Is there anything cheaper?

I'd like to confirm my reservation.

Chapter 2 Room Service

Wake-up Call

O : Operator.

P : Hello. I'd like a wake-up call, please.

O : For what time?

P : 6 o'clock(6 a.m), please.

O : What is your room number?

P : Fifteen seventeen.

O : O.K. Good night.

P : Thank you.

Room Service-Meal 1

W : Room service.

P : I'd like to order breakfast, please.

W : Sir. What would you like?

P : Two ham and eggs, toast and coffee.

W : All right, sir. I'll send it up right away. What is your room number?

P : Fifteen seventeen.

Room Service-Meal 2

W : Good morning. How are you?

P : I'm fine, thank you.

W : Would you like to have breakfast now?

P : Yes, please. I'll have an American Breakfast.

W : O.K. How would you like your eggs?

P : Scrambled, please.

Room Service-Transportation and Laundry

P : Hello. Room service? This is room fifteen seventeen. please call me a taxi.

W : All right, sir. That'll arrive about ten minutes.

P : You can call me, if they arrive in front of this hotel.

W : Sure.

....

P : Laundry service? I'd like to have two shirts washed.

L : Yes. I'll come up and by them. What's your room number?

P : Fifteen sixteen. Can I have them back by evening?

L : Yes. Around 6 o'clock, sir.

P : Thank you.

Room Service-Expressions

I'd like to order a snack, please.

May we have breakfast in our room

I'm still waiting for breakfast I ordered.

I'd like to have my laundry.

I want my shirts cleaned.

I'd like to have two shirts ironed. (pressed)

I'd like to have necktie dry cleaned.

When will they be ready?

Chapter 3 Check-Out

P : Hello. This is in room fifteen seventeen. Please send someone to bring down my baggage.

F : Are you checking out, sir?

P : Yes. I'll be right down. Would you please have my bill ready?

At the Front Desk

F : That will be one hundred and twenty-five dollars. Can you pay by cash or credit card?

P : By the way. May I pay by traveler's check?

F : Yes, you may.

P : My stay in your hotel has been very pleasant.

F : Thank you for staying with us, sir.

P : Good bye.

Leaving a Hotel

P : Good evening, I'll check out tomorrow morning about 8.

F : All right, sir. Your name and room number, please?

P : My name is Moon, fifteen sixteen.

F : O.K. We'll have your bill ready.

[Next Morning]

P : How much is the total bill?

F : That will be one hundred dollars. ($100.)

P : I'd like to pay for that with traveler's check.

F : Fine. I'm looking forward to seeing you again.

P : I'll try. Good bye.

Chapter 4 Hotel Restaurant

Reservation 1

P : Hello! I'd like to make a reservation for dinner.

W : Certainly, sir. When would you like to go?

P : Tonight, please.

W : For how many people?

P : For Five. How much will this cost?

W : Twenty dollars per person.

P : O.K. That's all.

W : Yes, we can. Thank you for calling. See you later, sir.

Reservation 2

P : Hello, Lady's Restaurant? I'd like to reserve a table at 7 this evening.

W : We're booked up that time. Could you make it at 7:30?

P : All right. we can. We'll be there at 7:30. Can I wear casual clothes?

W : Yes. sir. What's your name?

P : The name is Moon.

W : Right. Thank you for calling.

Reservation 3

P : I have a reservation. The name is Cheon.

W : Good evening, sir. Please come this way.

[Wine]

W : What would you like to drink wine, sir? We have Chablis. Moselle, California and Bordeaux wine.

P : Chablis wine, please.

W : Yes, sir.

....

P : Your Chablis wine. Would you like me to pour the wine?

W : Yes, please.

[Cocktail / Beer]

P : May I have the cocktail list, please?

W : Yes, sir. We have dry sherry, whisky soda, gin tonic scotch water, and strawberry.

P : Give me a glass of strawberry, please.

W : O.K. Just a moment, please.

[Waiter!......]

W : Did you call me? May I help you, sir?

T : What kind of beer do you have?

W : We have a Miller and Stout.

T : Give me a bottle of Stout

Giving an order 1

W : Are you ready to order now, sir?

P : Oh yes, We'll have two beef steaks, please.

W : Yes, sir. How would you like your steaks?

P : Well-done for the lady and medium for myself. Also can

we have a combination salad?

W : Yes, you can. What kind of dressing would you like?

P : Thousand island, please.

W : O.K. Thank you.

Giving an order 2

W : Do you have finished your dinner, sir?

P : Yes, I enjoyed it very much.

W : What would you like for dessert, sir? We have a choice of ice-cream or coffee.

P : Coffee, please.

Giving an order 3

P : Hello. Any tables available?

W : Please wait here for a few minutes.

......

W : Now we have a table for you. Please come this way.

P : Would you show me the menu, please?

W : Here you are. Would you like to order now, sir?

P : What's today's special menu?

W : We have Salmon with Smoked dish.

P : Salmon with Smoked dish, please.

[옆 사람에게 주문을 받으면서]

W : And you, sir?

T : I'd like to order a light meal. Do you have ham sandwich?

W : Yes, sir. What would you like to drink? We have orange juice, and coffee.

T : Orange juice, please.

W : Thank you very much.

Giving an order 4

W : Good morning, sir. What would you like for breakfast?

P : I'm fine, thank you. I'd like a piece of bread and coffee.

[American Breakfast]

W : And you, sir?

T : Two ham and eggs, bacon and coffee, please.

W : How would you like your eggs?

T : Sunny-side-up, please.

W : Thank you.

* hard-boiled egg 완숙

Giving an order 5

P : Two hamburger and one big hot dog, please.

W : For here or to go, sir?

P : To go, please.

W : What would you like on your hamburgers?

P : Sliced tomatoes, please.

W : Here you are. That'll be three dollars fifty cents.($3.50)

Giving an order 6

W : What would you like to drink, sir?

P : Give me a glass of Brandy, please.

W : All right, sir.

.....

P : Another one, please.

W : What would you like, sir?

T : Scotch on the rocks, please.

At the Counter

P : Waiter! check, please.

C : That'll be twenty-five dollars. You may pay by cash or credit card.

P : Can I pay by traveler's check?

C : Yes, you may.

P : I enjoyed it. Thank you very much.

Section 3 Tour Guide

Chapter 1 Transportation and Communication

Taxi 1

D : Where to, sir?

P : I'd like to go to Central Park.

D : Yes, sir. Are you in a hurry?

P : Yes, I must be there by one o'clock. I have an appointment with one of my American friend.

....

D : Here we are, sir.

P : How much do I owe you?

D : Eleven dollars.

P : Here you are. Keep the change, please.

D : Thank you.

Taxi 2

D : Where are you going, sir?

P : Downtown, please.

D : All right, sir. What part of downtown are you going?

P : Mall street, please.

D : Yes, sir.

P : But I want to stop at the Chicago building for a few minutes. How long does it take to go to Chicago building?

D : About thirty minutes. There is very much traffic.

Renting a car 1

P : Hi. I'd like to rent a car for two weeks.

C : What kind would you like?

P : An economy car, a compact.

C : May I see your international driver's license?

P : Yes, here it is.

C : Just fill out this form. Unlimited mileage and the mandatory collision insurance are included.

P : Do I have to return the car to this location?

C : No. You can drop it off at any of our local branches.

P : I see. Where is your car now?

C : It's in the parking lot.

Renting a car 2

P : I'd like to rent a car, please.

C : What kind would you like?

P : A small automatic, please.

C : May I see your international driver's license?

P : Yes, here it is.

C : How long do you want it for?

P : Four days. What is the rate?

C : Twenty-five dollars per day with unlimited mileage.

Car maintenance

Can you send a breakdown tow car?

The engine doesn't start.

Where's the nearest garage?

My car broke down on the highway. Send someone for it.

How long will it take to fix it?

Gas station

P : Fill it up with regular, please.

W : All right, sir.

P : Please check the water in the radiator.

W : The radiator's all right.

Where is the gas station? / I've run out of gasoline. / Check the oil, please.

* What would you like, sir, regular or premium?
* Regular and fill her up.

Bus 1

P : Does this bus stop at the downtown?

D : Yes. Get on, please.

P : How much is the fare?

D : Thirty cents.

P : I'm going to get off at Mall Department Store. Will you tell me when to get off?

D : Certainly.

Bus 2

P : Excuse me. Does this bus go to town center?

D : Yes, it does.

P : I want to go to the Mall Plaza. How many stops from here is it?

D : The fifth stop.

P : Thank you.

Bus 3

P : I'm going to get off at Hyde Park. How many stops from here is it?

D : You are on the wrong bus. Get off at the next stop and take bus number five.

Bus 4

P : I'd like to go to Chicago. Give me one ticket, please.

C : Is that one way or round trip?

P : One way ticket. What's the fare to Chicago?

C : 17 dollars.

P : Right. One ticket, please.

C : Here is your ticket.

P : Thank you very much.

Bus 5

Where is the bus stop?

What time will the next bus leave?

I get off at the next stop.

How many stops is it from here?

How often does the bus come?

Please let me know when we get there.

Where is the ticket office?

Do you have any medicine good for carsickness?

Train 1

P : I'd like to go to Gunsan. Is there an express train?

C : There is a 10:40 express.

P : When is the next train?

C : It leaves at 11:40

P : I'll take it. How much is the fare to Gunsan?

C : That will be twenty dollars.

P : Right. One ticket, please.

Train 2

Where's the booking office?

I want to reserve a seat on this train.

I'd like to reserve a berth. Up berth, please.

May I cancel this ticket?

I lost my ticket.

What time does the train arrive in Chicago?

Is this seat taken?

I lost my briefcase on this platform just a little while ago.

* berth 침대칸 / up berth 침대칸 위층

Subway

P : Excuse me. Can I go to Central Park by subway?

C : Yes, sir.

P : What's subway fare to Central Park?

C : The minimum fare is nineteen cents.

P : A one-way ticket, please. Where is the entrance?

C : Sure. Go straight ahead and you'll come right to it.

P : Thank you.

.....

P : How many train stop to Central Park?

W : The fifth stop.

Sea Transportation

P : Hello. I'd like to reserve a deck chair. How much is the fare to Mount Vernon.

C : Ten dollars thirty cents.

P : What time do we board?

C : At 11 a.m.

P : I feel like seasick. Do you have any medicine good for sea sickness?

Post Office 1

P : This letter needs to go by registered mail.

C : Where is it going?

P : To the Howon company.

C : Fill out this form and sign at the bottom.

P : Here you are.

C : O.K. That is 20 cents for the stamp and two dollars to send it by registered mail.

Post Office 2

P : I'd like to send this package to Korea by air.

C : What's in it?

P : They are all personal goods. Will you wrap this as a parcel?

C : Right. Would you fill out this form, please?

P : Will this do?

C : O.K. That is 80 cents for the stamp and thirty dollars to send it by parcel.

Collect Call

O : Operator. May I help you?

P : Hello. I would like to make a collect call, please.

O : What's the number and party's name?

P : Young-Soo Moon, 063-450-7443.

O : I need your name and room number, please

P : This is Jae-Yun, Cheon in fifteen seventeen.

O : Hang up and I'll call back. [later......]

O : Go ahead. Your party's on the line.

Phone Call 1

W : Good morning. Howon Company.

P : Hello May I speak to Prof. Moon, please?

W : I'm sorry, Prof. Moon is in a meeting at the moment.

Can he call you back?

P : Sure.

W : May I have your name and number, please?

P : Right. This is Prof. Cheon. I'm at 715-9064.

W : I'll have him call you right back.

Phone Call 2

W : Good morning. May I help you?

P : I'd like to speak to Prof. Cheon, please.

W : Sorry, he is off today.

P : I see. Do you know if he will be back in the office tomorrow?

W : He won't be back tomorrow. He is on vacation.

P : I'll call back later on.

Phone Call 3

P : Hello. Is Prof. Cheon in?

W : Sorry. Prof. Cheon just stepped away from his desk.

P : What time will he be back?

W : I'm sorry, but I have no idea. May I take a message?

P : Yes. Would you ask him to call Prof. Moon?

W : Right. Thank you for calling.

P : You're welcome.

Phone Call 4

P : Hello. Is this the Cheon's residence?

W : Yes.

P : This is Young-soo Moon. May I speak to Mr. Cheon, please?

W : Yes, Hold on, I'll get him.

P : Thank you.

[잠시후....]

P : Hello. This is Mr. Moon. I was wondering if you'd like to go out to dinner tonight?

T : That would be nice. What time should we meet?

P : Around 7. Is it too late for you?

T : No. I'll be ready!

Phone Call 5

W : Hello. Is Mr. Moon there?

M : There's no one here by that name. You have the wrong number.

W : I'm sorry to have bothered you.

M : That's all right.

Phone Call 6

Let me tell you my new phone number.

Hold on, please. I'll get a pencil.

I can't hear you. Would you speak more loudly?

Could you repeat that, please?

May I ask what this is in reference to?

Where is a public phone?

The line is busy.

Please call me up tomorrow morning.

Let me call you back later.

He will be back in a few minutes.

May I leave a message for him?

Would you answer the phone when it rings?

Chapter 2 Shopping and Exchange

Shopping 1

P : Excuse me. Could I have this one?

W : Just a moment, please. I'll be with you in a second.

P : I'd like to buy this camera.

W : You made an excellent selection. This is the largest selling brand.

P : How much is it?

W : One hundred and twenty dollars. Can you pay by cash or credit card?

P : By the way. May I pay by credit card?

W : Yes, you may.

Shopping 2

T : Please show me the one in the window?

W : What can I show you?

T : Would you show me that watch?

W : This one? How about this one?

T : O.K. I'll take it.

W : It is twenty dollars.

Shopping 3

W : What are you looking for?

P : No, thank you. I'm just looking around.

W : Yes, sir.

P : Excuse me. Would you show me this one?

W : This one? Purple bag are very popular this year.

P : Is it made of real leather?

W : Yes, it is.

P : How much is it?

W : Sixty dollars.

P : It's too expensive. Please show me a cheaper one.

W : O.K. How about this one?

P : (I don't like it.) I'll be back again.

Shopping 4

C : What are you looking for?

W : Excuse me. May I try this skirt on?

C : Oh, sure. The fitting room is right over here.

W : Thank you.

C : How does it fit?

W : It's little too tight. May I have a medium?

C : Right. I'll get it for you.

[A little later....]

W : Isn't the skirt a bit too long?

C : Yes. You look beautiful.

W : O.K. I'll take it. How much is it?

C : One hundred and thirty dollars. Can you pay by cash or credit card?

W : Traveler's check, please.

C : Fine. Sign it here.

Shopping 5

W : May I help you?

P : I'd like to see one of those ties.

W : You mean this one?

P : Yes.

W : It's pretty, isn't it? It's made of pure silk and is on sale.

P : O.K. I'll take it. Will you giftwrap it, please?

W : Could you take it to that counter, please?

Shopping 6

P : Do you carry perfume here?

W : We sure do. Which brand do you want?

P : I'd like to buy some Lotus Eau.

W : Yes, I'll get it for you.

P : O.K. I'll take it. How much is it?

W : Twenty dollars.

(잠시 옆 손님에게)

W : Hello. What are you looking for?

T : I'd like to buy a Guerlain Compact.

W : Over here, sir.

T : Fine. I'll take it. Please put it in a bag.

Shopping 7

W : How much is this Scotch?

C : Twenty dollars and sixth cents.

W : Can I pay by check?

C : I'm afraid you can't. We accept only traveler's checks and credit cards.

W : O.K. How about this card then?

P : We can take it. Please sign here.

Shopping 8

P : Do you carry books of poetry?

W : We sure do. What kind of poems are you interested in?

P : I like poems that tell us something.

W : Well, in that case I'd recommend the once on Shelf K-3 over there.

P : I'll take these two.

W : Thank you. I'll wrap up the books for you. I hope you'll enjoy reading them.

Shopping 9

P : Excuse me. I bought this just now and here's the receipt. I'm afraid I was short-changed. Could you look into it?

W : Oh, really? ......Sorry, here's the five I owe you. I'm terribly sorry.

Exchange 1

C : May I help you, sir?

P : Yes. I'd like to cash this travelers check.

C : How much would you like to cash?

P : Seventy dollars, please.

C : How do you want the money?

P : Twenty dollar bill, four tenners, two quarters, three

dimes, and four nickels.

C : Right. Sign it, please.

Exchange 2

C : May I help you, sir?

P : Yes. Can I have change for twenty dollar bill?

C : Sure.

P : Five quarters, six dimes, and three nickels, please.

C : Next, please. Good Morning, sir?

T : Would you please change some dollar bills?

C : Yes, sir. How do you want the money?

T : Small change, please.

Chapter 3 Sightseeing

Sightseeing Information 1

W : Good morning. May I help you?

P : I'd like to see some of city's sights. Do you have any tour to Chicago?

W : Sure. Are you taking a tour today?

P : Yes. How much is it per person?

W : Twenty-five dollars.

Sightseeing Information 2

W : Have you seen much of Disneyland?

P : Yes.

W : Did you go to the National Museum, too?

P : I did. There were lots of things to see. I might go there again before I leave.

W : Good idea. What else did you see?

P : I saw a folk dance at the National Theater the other night.

W : How did you like that?

P : Very much. It was a wonderful show.

Ballon Riding

P : Excuse me. Sorry to bother you, but could you tell me where I can buy ticket for balloon riding?

W : Go to Box C on the third floor.

P : I'd like two tickets for the next balloon ride, please.

C : The tickets for the 2:30 flight are all sold out, and the next flight will be at 3:30. Will that be all right?

P : O.K. Balloon riding must be very popular.

C : It's getting more and more popular. Here are your tickets. That'll be four dollars.

P : O.K. Here you are.

C : Have a good time.

P : Thank you.

Sightseeing Expressions

I'd like to get a city map, please.

Do you have any sightseeing program?

Is lunch included?

I'd like to see some of the city's nightfall.

Do you have any tour to Disneyland?

Do you have a sightseeing brochure?

I'm going to see New York on my own.

What's that building over there?

I'd like to see some places of interest.

Do you know what that is?

Do you know where I can go and return in a day?

Taking a picture 1

P : Excuse me. Would you please take our picture?

W : Sure. Where would you like to stand?

P : Stand right here, please. You may just push the button.

W : O.K. Smile. Good.

P : Thank you very much.

Taking a picture 2

P : Excuse me. May I take a picture of you with your children?

W : Sure.

P : Smile....Cheese!..... I'll mail it to you. Tell me your address please.

W : Thank you. I hope it comes out good.

Taking a picture – Expressions

I need a roll of film for my camera.

Will you take our picture?

I want you to join us, if you don't mind.

Can you focus the camera?

I need to develop my negatives.

How much do you charge for developing?

This camera doesn't work. Can you repair it?

Chapter 4 Directions

Directions 1

P : Excuse me. I'm lost. Could you tell me the way to the Mall Center?

W : Sure. Just go straight along this street and turn right at the next corner.

P : How long will it take?

W : Oh, only a few minutes.

P : Thanks a lot.

Directions 2

P : We're completely lost. Where are we now?

W : I'm sorry. I'm a stranger here.

P : Here comes a officer. Let's ask him. Excuse me. May I ask where we're now?

O : Yes, you're right in the middle of fifth Avenue.

P : Please point out where I am on this map:

O : All right.

Directions 3

P : Excuse me. Can you direct me to the toy department, please?

W : It's on the 5th floor. As you get off the elevator, you'll see it on your right.

P : Can you direct me to the elevator?

W : Sure. Go straight ahead and you'll come left to it.

P : Thank you very much.

Directions 4 – Expressions

Which way to the hotel?

How long will it take me to get there?

Could you draw me a sketch, please?

How long does it take on foot?

Where do you want to go?

How far is it from here?

Where can I find a police box?

Is it in this direction?

Excuse me. Can you tell me where the rest room is?

Is it on the left or right?

Turn left at the end of the hall.

It's three blocks straight ahead. You can't miss it.

Chapter 5 Amusement

Movie

W : Go straight along this street. The movie theater is opposite the post office.

....

C : Hello. May I help you?

P : What films are on now?

C : Action movie.

P : What's the admission price?

C : Seven dollars. What kind of seats do you like?

P : I want a front seat, please.

Theater

P : What's on tonight?

W : We have Spider woman play.

P : What time does the curtain go up?

W : At 7 o'clock.

Concert

P : I'd like to buy an advance ticket for the concert by the Moscow Symphony Orchestra.

W : What kind of seats do you like?

P : I want a seat in the gallery.

Expressions

Where can I see an opera?

Are today's tickets still available?

Where can I get a ticket?

Would you like to go to the concert?

Can I have a seat for today?

How much are the tickets?

Could you tell me what musical is playing today?

Can you recommend a film?

Which film is popular?

Let's go to the movies tonight.

Chapter 6 Leisure and Sports

Watching a game

P : I'd like to see a basket-ball game. Can I still get a ticket?

W : Sure

P : What's the admission price?

W : Five dollars. What kind of seats do you like?

P : I want a front seat, please.

Swimming

P : Excuse me. What time does the swimming pool close?

W : At 5 o'clock. Did you bring your bathing suit?

P : Yes. How deep is the pool?

W : It's not too deep.

Jet-skiing

P : I'd like to rent this jet skis. How much is it?

W : Five dollars.

P : I've never tried one. Can you teach me how to drive?

W : Sure. Just a moment, please.

Expressions

I want some information about basket-ball games.

Where can I get a ticket?

Is it possible to ski at this time of the year?

Lend me a fishing tackle, please.

How much must I pay per hour?

I don't have a reservation. Can we play some golf?

Do you have your own clubs?

How much is the green fee?

Chapter 7 Crisis Management

Illness 1

D : Sorry I kept you waiting. I'm Dr. Kram.

P : Good afternoon. Dr. Kram. I've heard a lot about you. People are speaking highly of you.

D : Are they? I'm glad to hear that. Well, what's the trouble?

P : I have a bad headache, and a sore throat, too.

D : Let me see. It's a bad cold. Nothing serious, though.

P : Am I going to be all right soon?

D : You'll be all right by Wednesday, I think. Now the nurse will give you a shot and some pills.

P : Thank you very much.

D : Take care, Moon.

Illness 2

D : Well, what's the trouble?

P : I have a stomachache.

D : Nothing serious, though. I'll prescribe some medicine for your stomach.

P : Thank you very much.

(잠시 후)

P : Some stomach medicine, please.

D : Do you have the prescription?

P : Yes. I have.

Illness 3

D : What's the matter?

P : I've got a pain in my ankle.

D : Nothing is the matter with the bone.

P : Thank you very much.

How's your appetite?

Give me a peptic, please.

Take me to the hospital, please.

Accident 1

P : I lost my traveler's checks.

C : Did you remember where you lose them?

P : I was not sure.

C : Do you have the record with the check numbers.

P : Yes. Here it is. When can I have them reissued?

C : Just a moment, please.

Accident 2

W : What can I do for you?

P : I lost my bag on this platform just a little while ago.

W : What kind of bag is it?

P : It's brown bag.

W : How can we contact you, if we find your bag?

Expressions

Where is lost and found office?

Where should I come to get it?

Could you please look for it?

Where shall we send it for you, if we find it?

I lost my passport.

Where did you lose it?

Please reissue my passport.

Where did you put it?

I left my bag in the taxi.

[부록 1] 관광가이드 영어회화

기내에서

Would you please show me how to fasten this belt?
이 벨트를 어떻게 착용하는지 좀 가르쳐 주시겠습니까?

How much do I owe you?
얼마를 지불해야 합니까?

Excuse me. I feel sick. Please give me some medicine.
죄송하지만 몸이 좋지 않은데. 약 좀 주시겠습니까?

What kind of drink do you have?
음료수는 어떤 종류가 있습니까?

What will you drink? = What would you like to drink?
무엇을 마시겠습니까?

Do you have any newspapers?
신문은 있습니까?

Do you have airsickness medicine?
멀미약이 있습니까?

Do you have any cigarettes?
혹시 담배 있습니까?

May I change my seat?
자리를 바꿔도 됩니까?

May I sit here?
이 자리에 앉아도 됩니까?

May I smoke?
담배를 피워도 됩니까?

Can I have a glass of ice water?
얼음물 한 잔 주세요?

I feel like throwing out.
토할 것 같아요.

May I go to the toilet now?
화장실에 갈 수 있습니까?

공항관련(입국심사, 비행기 예약, 확인 등)

A : Your passport, please. = Please show me your passport.
B : Here you are. = Here it is.
A : 여권을 보여 주십시오.
B : 여기 있습니다.

Please fill in this form.
이 용지를 기재해 주세요.

Where are you from? = What is your nationality?
국적이 어디입니까?

What's the purpose of your visit (stay / trip)?
방문(체재 / 여행) 목적이 무엇입니까?

I am travelling for sightseeing. = travelling
관광 여행 중입니다.

I am here on a tour.
관광으로 왔습니다.

I am here on studying. = studying
공부하러 왔습니다.

I am here to visit my friends.
친구를 만나러 왔습니다.

How long are you staying? = How long are you going to stay?
얼마 동안 체류하실 예정입니까?

A : Anything to declare?

B : Just my personal effects(things).

I have nothing to declare. = No, nothing.

I have something to declare.

Is this all you have?

A : 신고하실 것이 있습니까?
B : 제 개인 휴대품뿐입니다.
신고할 물건이 없습니다.
네 있습니다.
짐은 이것뿐입니까?

What kind of job?

당신의 직업은 무엇입니까?

Where do I pick up my baggage from the UA flight 820?

UA 820 편의 짐은 어디서 찾을 수 있습니까?

Do they have through plane to springfield?

스프링필드로 가는 직행 비행기가 있나요?

I have to change flights in Chicago.

시카고에서 갈아타야 합니다.

Book me for the 4:20 flight, please.

4시 20분 항공편에 예약해 주세요.

The 4:20 flight is sold out.

4시 20분 항공편은 매진되었습니다.

I'll take the 2 PM flight.

오후 2시 비행기로 하겠습니다.

One way ticket or return?

편도입니까, 왕복입니까?

When would you like?

언제 출발하시겠습니까?

We can give you a seat on August 30.

8월 30일에는 빈 좌석이 있습니다.

What's the fare?

항공 요금은 얼마지요?

Charge it, please.

크레디트 카드로 지불하겠습니다.

I'd like to change flights.

항공편을 변경하려고 합니다.

Is this the reservation office?

예약 접수처입니까?

I want to reserve a seat from Paris to Seoul.

파리와 서울간의 좌석을 예약하고 싶은데요.

I want to reconfirm my reservation.

예약을 재확인하고 싶습니다.

How do you spell your first name?

이름의 스펠링을 말해 주시겠어요?

I'd like to cancel my reservation for the flight on July 25, and book on July 30 instead, please.

7월 25일 예약을 취소하고 대신 7월30일로 부탁드립니다.

I'd like to book a flight to Los Angeles, and purchase the ticket.

LA가는 비행기를 예약하고 항공권을 구하려고 합니다.

Would you like to book your return flight, too?

돌아오는 비행기 편도 예약하시겠습니까?

What class would you like? economy, business or first?

어떤 좌석을 원하나요? 일반석, 이등석, 아니면 일등석?

Business class, please.

이등석으로 주세요.

Is the plane on schedule?

비행기는 예정대로 운행됩니까?

Where do I check in?

탑승 수속은 어디서 합니까?

What time do we board (the plane)?
비행기 탑승은 몇 시에 시작됩니까?

Boarding will begin at 1:20 at Gate 12.
탑승은 1시 20분, 12번 창구에서 시작됩니다.

I'm in transit to …
저는 …행 비행기로 갑니다.

I have a plane to catch at two.
2시에 비행기를 타야 합니다.

Would you like to sit in the non-smoking or the smoking section?
금연석을 원하세요, 아니면 흡연석을 원하세요?

Window seat or aisle?
창문가를 원하세요, 아니면 통로 쪽을 원하세요?

How many pieces of baggage would you like to check?
맡기실 짐은 몇 개인가요?

May I see your disembarkation card?
입국 카드를 보여 주시겠습니까?

How long are you staying?
어느 정도 머물 예정입니까?

Where are you staying?
어디서 머물 예정입니까?

What's your final destination?
최종 목적지가 어디입니까?

I didn't get a quarantine card.
검역 카드를 받지 않았습니다.

숙소에서 (호텔, 호스텔 등)

Have you made a reservation?
예약을 하셨습니까?

Do you have a room available?
빈 방이 있습니까?

How long will you be staying?
얼마 동안 이곳에 묵으실 겁니까?

What's the check-out time?
체크아웃 시간이 몇 시죠?

How do I call Room Service?
룸서비스를 부를 때는 어떻게 하지요?

Will you break this bill?
이 지폐를 잔돈으로 바꿔주시겠습니까?

I'm checking out now.
지금 퇴숙하려고 합니다.

How can I make an international call?
국제전화를 걸려면 어떻게 하면 되죠?

I'd like to check in. please.
체크인을 하고 싶습니다.

Would you fill out this registration card, please?
이 숙박카드에 기입해 주세요.

Hot water doesn't come out in my bath tub.
욕조의 더운 물이 나오지 않습니다.

When is breakfast?
아침식사 시간은 언제입니까?

When does the dining room open?
식당은 몇 시에 문을 엽니까?

I'd like to make reservations.
예약하려고 합니다.

I'd like a room for one.
싱글 침대 방으로 부탁합니다.

Fill this out and sign here, please.
여기에 기재하시고 사인하세요.

You have until six o'clock to cancel this reservation.
이 예약을 취소하려면 6시까지 전화해 주세요.

What kind of room would you like, sir?
어떤 방이 필요합니까?

I'd like a quiet room.
조용한 방으로 부탁합니다.

Could we get a room with a view of the beach?
해변이 보이는 방으로 부탁합니다.

I want a room with a nice view.
전망이 좋은 방으로 부탁합니다.

I'll take this room.
이 방으로 하겠습니다.

I'll stay three nights.
3일 밤 머물 겁니다.

It's too expensive for me.
내게는 너무 비쌉니다.

Is there anything cheaper?
좀 더 싼 방은 없습니까?

Is breakfast included?
요금은 아침 식사 포함입니까?

I'd like to check my baggage.
짐을 맡기고 싶어요.

Can I leave my camera with you?
내 카메라를 맡기고 싶은데요.

Do you have any other valuables to deposit?
맡기실 다른 귀중품은 없습니까?

Can I extend my stay two more days?
숙박을 이틀 더 연기할 수 있습니까?

I'd like my valuable back.
맡긴 귀중품을 돌려주세요.

Do you think I can stay tonight?
오늘 이곳에서 묵을 수 있을까요?

How much for a night?
하루에 얼마에요?

I want to stay for two nights.
2박을 하고 싶습니다.

Can I cook for myself?
취사를 할 수 있나요?

길 묻기

I'm a stranger here.
나는 이곳이 초행입니다.

How can I get there?
그 곳에는 어떻게 갑니까?

Is it far away? = Is it far from here?
거리가 멉니까?

It's a 15-minute ride.
차로 15분 거리입니다.

It's within walking distance.
걸어서 갈만한 거리입니다.

Where are we now?
여기가 어디죠?

Keep straight on.
앞으로 곧장 가십시오.

How far is it to the Effel Tower?

에펠 탑까지는 얼마나 멉니까?

Where is the nearest subway station?

가장 가까운 지하철역이 어디 있습니까?

Where can I find a public telephone?

공중전화가 어디 있습니까?

Excuse me, Please. Is there a department store near by?

죄송하지만 이 부근에 백화점이 있습니까?

I've lost my way.

길을 잃었습니다.

I'd like to go to subway station.

지하철역으로 가고 싶습니다.

Excuse me, but can you show me the way to the station?

but could you tell me where the station is?

but could you tell me how to get to the station?

미안합니다만, 역으로 가는 길을 가리켜 주시겠습니까?

Where's the rest room, please? = Where can I wash my hands?

화장실이 어딥니까?

May I use the rest room?

화장실을 좀 써도 됩니까?

Can I get some directions?

길 좀 가리켜 주시겠어요?

Go down this street and make a right at the first light.

첫 번째 신호등에서 오른 쪽으로 도세요.

Could you direct me to the post office?

= Tell me how to get to the post office, please.

= Could you show me the way to the post office?

우체국 가는 길을 가르쳐 주세요.

Is there a post here around here?

이 근처에 우체국이 어디 있습니까?

Can I walk there?
걸어가도 됩니까?

How long will it take to walk there?
걸어가는 데 얼마나 걸립니까?

What street is this?
이 거리는 뭐라고 부릅니까?

Are we there yet?
거의 다 왔습니까?

Where is your parking lot?
주차장이 어디 있습니까?

Where can I buy a ticket?
차표는 어디에서 살 수 있습니까?

Where can I catch a bus to go to New York?
뉴욕 행 버스는 어디에서 탑니까?

Toilet / Wash Room / Bath Room Powder Room
Lavatory / Rest Room / W.C. (= Water Closet)
화장실

은행 관련

Excuse me. Where can I change some money?
실례하겠습니다. 어디서 환전합니까?

I'd like to cash this traveler's check.
이 여행자 수표를 현금으로 좀 바꿔주세요.

Small change, Please.
소액으로 주십시오.

I'd like to have these checks cashed.
이 수표를 현금으로 교환하려 합니다.

How would you like to have the money?
= How do you like(want) to have the money?
어떤 돈으로 드릴까요?

Two 5 dollar bill and ten one dollar bill, Please.
5달러짜리 2장, 1달러짜리 열 장으로 부탁합니다.

Please change this bill into small money?
이 지폐를 잔돈으로 바꾸어 주십시오.

Give me the change, please.
거스름돈 주세요.

I'd like change for a ten, please.
10달러 지폐를 바꾸어 주세요.

Can you change some Pound into dollars, please?
파운드를 달러로 바꾸어 줄 수 있습니까?

How late is the bank open?
은행은 몇 시까지 합니까?

I'd like some small change?
잔돈도 주세요.

I want it all in singles.
전부 1달러로 주세요.

What's the exchange rate today?
오늘의 외환시세는 얼마입니까?

What rate of commission do you charge?
수수료는 얼마입니까?

교통편 이용

Which bus goes downtown?
어느 버스가 시내로 갑니까?

When's the bus coming?
버스는 언제 옵니까?

Let me know where to get off.
어디서 내려야 하는지 알려 주십시오.

When is the next bus for Phoenix?
피닉스 행 다음 버스는 언제 있습니까?

Please show me how to get there?
그곳으로 가는 방법을 가르쳐 주십시오.

Where do I change? = Where should I transfer?
어디서 갈아타야 합니까?

Where's the bus stop, please?
버스 정류장은 어디입니까?

Please give me two tickets to Boston.
보스톤 가는 표 2장 주세요.

Which kind of train do you want take?
어떤 종류의 열차로 하시겠습니까?

Excuse me. Is this seat free? (Is this seat vacant?)
이 자리는 비어 있습니까?

Excuse me. Is this seat occupied? (Is this seat taken?)
이 자리는 차 있습니까?

Where are we passing now?
지금 어디를 지나고 있습니까?

식당에서

May I take your order, please?

주문을 받을까요?

Yes, please.

네.

Just a moment, please. I haven't made up my mind yet.

잠깐만 기다려 주세요. 아직 정하지 않았습니다.

Same here.

저도 같은 걸로 주십시오.

I want my steak well-done.

스테이크를 완전히 익혀서 주세요.

What would you like to drink?

음료수는 무엇을 드시겠습니까?

I'll try it.

그것을 먹어보겠습니다.

Excuse me. Waiter! May I order now?

주문을 하고 싶은데요.

I'm just about finished. Check, please.

식사가 끝났어요. 계산서 갖다 주세요.

Would you like separate checks?

두 분 따로 계산할까요?

No, one check, please.

아니, 같이 해 주세요.

You gave me wrong change.

거스름돈이 틀립니다.

물건사기

I'd like to buy a handbag.

핸드백 하나를 사려고 합니다.

I'm just looking around. = I'm just browsing around.

그냥 구경하는 중입니다.

This is too expensive for me.

이것은 너무 비싼 것 같군요.

Can you give me a discount a little?

= Can you come down a little?

좀 할인해 줄 수 있습니까?

Please show me a cheaper one.

좀 더 싼 것을 보여 주세요.

I think I'll take this one.

이것을 사도록 하겠습니다.

I'll take it.

그것을 사겠습니다.

May(Can) I try it on?

입어 봐도 되겠습니까?

How much (are they in all)?

모두 얼마입니까?

Do you accept traveler's checks?

여행자 수표를 받습니까?

Please show me that.

저것을 보여 주세요.

Do you have any other one?

다른 물건 있습니까?

Don't you have any other size?

다른 사이즈 없습니까?

Do you have this in a larger size?
좀 더 큰 사이즈는 없습니까?

Does this price include tax?
이 가격은 세금이 포함된 것입니까?

Can I get it tax-free?
면세로 살 수 있습니까?

I like this one. I'll take it.
이것이 마음에 듭니다. 그것을 주십시오.

관광을 즐길 때

Please tell me some of the Places I should visit.
꼭 구경해야 할 곳 몇 군데를 가르쳐 주십시오.

How much is the fare?
입장료가 얼마입니까?

Is it permitted to take pictures?
여기서 사진 찍는 것이 허락됩니까?

Can I take picture here?
여기서 사진 찍어도 됩니까?

I'm sorry you can't take pictures here.
여기서는 촬영할 수 없습니다.

Excuse me, but would you please press this shutter for me?
죄송하지만 셔터를 좀 눌러주시겠습니까?

Will you take a picture with me?
함께 사진을 찍을 수 있습니까?

Will you take a picture of me with this camera?
이 카메라로 사진을 좀 찍어 주시겠습니까?

관광안내소 이용 시

Is there a photo service around here?
이 근처에 사진관이 있습니까?

Do you have that tour everyday?
그 관광은 매일 출발합니까?

What can I see on the tour?
그 관광에서 무엇을 볼 수 있습니까?

Do you have a night tour?
야간 관광이 있습니까?

Are there any city sightseeing bus?
시내 관광버스는 있습니까?

How long does it take?
시간이 얼마나 걸립니까?

Are any meals included?
식사 포함입니까?

How much is this tour?
이 관광은 얼마입니까?

Where can I buy a ticket?
표는 어디서 삽니까?

Please give me a tour pamphlet.
관광 안내서를 주세요.

Do you have map of this city?
이 도시의 지도가 있습니까?

I want to get a map of the subway lines.
지하철의 지도가 있습니까?

Will you suggest some interesting places to visit on the city?
이곳의 구경거리를 가르쳐 주세요?

일상영어

How's it going? / How's you doing? / How's everything going?
안녕하세요.

Fine. And you? / How about yourself?
네. 당신은 어떠세요?

See you.
또 만납시다.

Take care.
조심하세요.

You're welcome.
천만의 말씀.

Please help me.
좀 도와주세요.

Please wait a minute. / Just a moment, please.
잠깐만 기다려주세요.

I have to hurry.
저는 서둘러야 합니다.

I have a problem.
어려운 문제 한 가지 있습니다.

A: Where are you from?
B: I came from Korea. (= I'm from Korea)
A : 국적이 어디입니까? (= 어디서 오셨습니까?)
B : 한국에서 왔습니다.

Please say it again.
다시 말씀해주세요.

I can't hear you.
잘 들리지 않습니다.

May I have some water?
물 좀 주시겠습니까?

May I borrow your pen?

펜 좀 빌릴까요?

I think so.

그렇게 생각합니다.

I don't think so.

그렇게 생각하지 않습니다.

I'm sorry, I don't know.

죄송하지만 잘 모르겠습니다.

Don't mention it. / Think nothing of it.

그런 말씀 마세요.

My pleasure.

제가 좋아서 한 겁니다.

It's nothing.

별 것 아닙니다.

Any time.

언제라도 부탁하세요.

I appreciate your offer but you don't have to go to that trouble.

말씀은 고맙지만, 그렇게 수고하실 필요가 없습니다.

It's a token of my appreciation for your kind assistance.

이것은 당신이 친절히 도와주신데 대한 감사의 표시입니다.

Thank you for the tip.

가르쳐 주셔서 고맙습니다.

Thank you for your time.

시간을 내 주셔서 감사합니다.

All right.

좋습니다.

That's will be fine.

그것으로 좋습니다.

After you.

당신 먼저.

Nice day, isn't it?
좋은 날씨군요.

I had a good time.
매우 즐거웠습니다.

I'm going to Los Angeles. And you?
나는 LA로 가는 길입니다. 당신의 목적지는?

What is your business? / What is your occupation?
당신의 직업은 무엇입니까?

Have you ever traveled in Korea?
한국을 여행한 적이 있습니까?

I wish you would.
부디 한 번 와 주세요.

I surely will, if I have a chance.
기회가 있으면 꼭 가고 싶습니다.

May I ask your name?
당신의 이름은 무엇입니까?

Could you spell it for me, please?
이름의 철자를 말씀해 주시겠어요?

Please speak more slowly.
좀 더 천천히 말씀해 주세요.

Can I sit here?
여기 앉아도 좋습니까?

I'm looking for …
…을 찾고 있습니다.

How much is this?
이것은 얼마입니까?

What time is it?
몇 시입니까?

It's a quarter to ten.
10시 15분 전입니다.

What day is it today?

오늘 무슨 요일입니까?

What's the occasion?

오늘이 무슨 날이지?

Could I trouble you for a light?

실례지만 불가진 것 있습니까?

여행영어

May I see your boarding pass, please?

탑승권을 좀 보여 주시겠습니까?

What can I do with this bag, Mr?

이 가방을 어떻게 할 까요?

Please put it under your seat or in the overhead bin.

의자 밑이나 머리 위에 있는 통 속에 놓아두십시오.

How many more hours until we land in New York?

몇 시간 더 가면 뉴욕에 착륙합니까?

How much farther is it?

얼마나 더 가야 되죠?

What time do we land in Chicago?

몇 시에 시카고에 착륙할까요?

Are you going to serve dinner on this flight?

비행 중에 저녁식사가 나옵니까?

What's the purpose of your visit?

방문 목적은 무엇입니까?

When do you plan to return to your home country?

고국에 언제 돌아가실 계획입니까?

How long are you going to stay in this country?

이 나라에 얼마동안 머물 예정이십니까?

Take me to the Sheraton Hotel in Manhattan.
맨하탄의 쉐라톤 호텔까지 부탁합니다.

How far is it from here?
여기서 거리가 얼마나 되지요?

It'll take maybe thirty minutes this time of night.
밤 이맘때면 아마 30분쯤 걸릴 겁니다.

About how much will the fare be?
요금은 얼마나 될까요?

How long will it take?
시간은 얼마나 걸릴까요?

I have to catch a plane. Can't you hurry?
비행기를 타야 하는데요. 급히 갈 수 없을까요?

I'm going as fast as I can.
최선을 다해서 가고 있습니다.

Do you have a single room available?
일인용 방이 있습니까?

When are you checking in?
언제 들어오시죠?

For how many nights, sir?
며칠 밤을 주무실 겁니까, 손님?

I'd like to stay 3 nights and check out Saturday morning.
삼일 밤을 지내고 토요일 오전에 나가려고요.

I'd like a room, please.
방 하나 있습니까?

Single or double, sir?
1인용을 말씀하십니까, 아니면 2인용을 말씀하십니까?

The porter will take your bags.
짐꾼이 가방을 운반해 드릴 겁니다.

Are you checking in now?
지금 들어오시겠습니까?

What is the check-out time?
방을 나가야 하는 시간이 언제입니까?

I'll be checking out tomorrow morning at eight.
내일 아침 8시에 나가게 될 겁니다.

My room is too close to the elevator. Can I change it?
내 방이 엘리베이터에 너무 가까이 있는데 바꿀 수 있을까요?

Sorry, sir. We're full. / I'm sorry we're all booked up. /
I'm sorry, but we have no vacancy.
죄송합니다. 방이 만원입니다.

Sorry, sir. Nothing else is vacant.
미안합니다. 손님. 그거 말고는 빈방이 하나도 없어요.

Can you give me a wake-up call at six?
6시에 내방으로 전화를 해서 좀 깨워 주시겠어요?

Hang on. I'll transfer your call to the front desk.
잠시만 기다리세요. 프론트 데스크로 전화를 돌려드리겠습니다.

Could you suggest some interesting places to visit?
관광할 만한 데를 몇 군데 소개해 주시겠습니까?

Can you break a twenty dollar bill?
20불짜리뿐인데 잔돈으로 거슬러 주시겠어요?

Sure, if you don't mind getting a lot of singles.
물론이죠. 1불짜리 여러 개로 드려도 괜찮으시다면.

I can break it for you.
제가 거슬러 들릴 수 있습니다.

You have to pay in advance.
미리 지불하셔야 합니다.

I'd better call and reserve the tickets in advance.
전화를 해서 표를 미리 예약해야겠습니다.

We have about five more hours to go.
5시간쯤 더 가면 돼요.

Fill her (it) up. Unleaded, please.

무연으로 한 탱크 가득 채워 주세요.

Do you want me to check your oil and water?

기름과 물도 점검해 드릴까요?

Is this pump self-service?

여기는 본인이 직접 기름을 넣는 곳인가요?

Self-service is a few cents cheaper per gallon than Full-service.

셀프서비스는 풀 서비스보다 갤런 당 몇 센트가 저렴해요.

Do you want your car washed?

세차를 원하세요?

I hear you're (returning) going to L.A.

L.A.에 (돌아)가신다면서요.

When are you leaving?

언제 떠나십니까?

How are you going?

언제 떠나십니까?

Are you flying?

비행기로 가시나요?

Where are you headed?

어디 가십니까?

I'm on my way to New York.

뉴욕에 가는 중입니다.

I have four weeks off for vacation.

4주간 휴가 입니다.

What's your destination?

목적지가 어디신가요?

Which street am I on now?

지금 여기가 몇 가 입니까?

How do I get to the post office from here?

여기서 우체국을 어떻게 갑니까?

It's three blocks north on Clark Street.
클락 스트리트에서 북쪽으로 세 블록에 있습니다.

Which way do I go to get to Clark Street?
클락 스트리트를 가려면 어느 쪽으로 가야 합니까?

You are on Clark Street.
지금 여기가 클락 스트리트입니다.

How far is the Museum from here?
여기서 박물관까지는 얼마나 멉니까?

It's about two blocks from here.
여기서 약 2블록 정도입니다.

Where are you from?
고향이 어디세요?

Seoul is famous for its Seoul Tower.
서울은 서울 타워로 유명합니다.

The traffic was bumper to bumper this morning.
오늘 아침에 교통이 굉장히 복잡했어요.

How long does it take?
시간이 얼마나 걸리나?

I left my house at the usual time and it took two hours to get here.
보통 때와 같은 시각에 집을 떠났는데 여기까지 2시간이나 걸렸어요.

How often do you have flights to New York?
얼마나 자주 뉴욕행 비행기가 있습니까?

Would you mind if I sit here?
여기 앉아도 될까요?

Do you want to join us?
우리하고 같이 갈래?

Have you waited to long?
오래 기다리셨어요?

Does it matter much if I go?

내가 가면 아주 곤란한가요?

Would you care for something to drink?

마실 것 좀 드릴까요?

Would you mind trading seats with me?

기내에서 좌석을 바꾸고 싶을 때

I feel sick. / I feel like vomiting.

몸이 아플 때(멀미가 날 때)

Could I have a blanket?

담요가 필요할 때

I have nothing to declare.

세관에 신고할 물품이 없을 때

What brought you?

입국목적을 물을 때

I am here on vacation.

여행목적을 말 할 때

Could you put me in the no-smoking section.

금연석을 희망할 때

How long are you staying?

며칠이나 머물 계획이냐

What's the rate?

택시 요금을 물을 때

Is there a room available tonight?

오늘 묵을 방이 있습니까?

Is breakfast included?

아침 식사는 제공되나요?

Let me off here, please.

차에서 내리고 싶을 때

A one-way to Seoul, please.

서울행 편도 1장 주세요.

Please let me know when I get to Seoul.
(차장에게) 서울에 도착하면 알려 주세요.

I'd like to check in, please.
체크인 하고 싶습니다.

I'd like a twin room, please.
트윈 룸에 묵고 싶습니다.

What's the rate for a twin room?
트윈 룸은 얼마죠?

I locked myself out.
열쇠를 방안에 놓아두고 방문을 닫았을 때

May I have some water, please?
물을 마시고 싶을 때

I'm just looking.
(상점 등에서) 그냥 구경하는 겁니다.

Can't you make it a little cheaper?
(물건을 살 때) 싸게 해 주세요.

[부록 2] Tour Guide about Korea

Seoul

Seoul is both the capital and the heart of the Republic of Korea, containing about 10.2 million of the nation's 44.6 million people. It is the financial, political, commercial, recreational, educational, and cultural center of Korea, home to major corporations, banks, government offices, leading schools and universities.

Everland

It is two amusement parks in one. Its Festival World has thrilling rides, a jungle safari and zoo, and seasonal flower festivals. And Caribbean Bay is a huge water park with wave pools and water slides.

Seoul Land

It is an all-weather theme park which can be reached in 20 minutes from downtown Seoul. Here 40 kinds of amusement facilities await visitors. Colorful events and seasonal fairs create fun and spectacles.

Admiral Yi Sun-shin

Admiral Yi Sun-shin is the historic war hero of Korea, similar in importance to Admiral Nelson of the United kingdom. At the end of the 16th century, when there were two great wars against the invading Japanese.

Jejudo

Jejudo, one of the nine provinces of Korea, is only an hour's flight south of Seoul and less than that from Busan or Daegu. It has a mild marine climate. It has four distinct seasons and an average yearly temperature of 15℃. It also has become a favorite retreat with honeymooners and tourists.

Taekwondo

Taekwondo originated in Korea and is now officially recognized around the world. It is a whole-body sport which uses the arms and legs in particular.

Hanbok

The hanbok has been the Korean people's unique traditional costume for thousands of years. The beauty and grace of Korean culture can be seen in photographs of women dressed in the hanbok.

Itaewon

Itaewon is a popular shopping district especially for foreign tourists. It is becoming internationally more famous as the years go by.

Gyongbokgung Palace

This palace was first built in 1935 by King Taejo, the founder of the Yi Dynasty, but was burned during the Japanese invasion of 1592. It was rebuilt in 1868.

Doksugung Palace

This palace is located along the west side of Seoul City Hall Plaza. It was originally a royal villa but later used by King Gojong as his residence until his death in 1919.

Insa-dong

Many traditional Korean products delight tourists. They include ceramics, scrolls, old folk items and various antique furniture. You can find these things in Insa-dong.

Korean Folk Village

The Folk Village is about an hour's drive south from Seoul. In the village there are reconstructed farm houses and noble mansions, an outdoor marketplace as well as an amusement park.

Mt. Sorak National Park

This park consists of 344 square kilometers. The area is divided geographically into the Inner and Outer area.

Chomsongdae Observatory

Chomsongdae was actually used for observing the stars. according to recent research, this 9.2 meter structure was built based on complex mathematical principles.

Calligraphy

Calligraphy is a refined art form in Korea, as in China and Japan. Attaining writing proficiency takes years of training.

Panmunjom

Panmunjom is located in the middle of the Demilitarized Zone(DMZ), an hour and a half by bus to the north of Seoul.

Hangul

Koreans have their own unique alphabet called hangul. It is considered to be one of the most efficient and scientific alphabets in the world.

Korean Ginseng

Ginseng is a medicinal plant. It is a perennial herb. Korean-grown ginseng has special medicinal powers. It isi used as a restorative or tonic, rather than as a cure for a particular illness.

Gimchi

Throughout the world Gimchi is known as the traditional Koran pickled vegetable dish. Not only is Gimchi rich in various nutrients, but the science of preparing Gimchi makes it very unique food.

References

문영수 · 천재윤(2005). 누워서 보는 영어, 백산출판사.

문영수 · 천재윤(2005). 크게 웃고 가는 리딩스킬, 백산출판사.

문영수 · 천재윤(2010). Grammar Free Zone, 백산출판사.

문영수 · 천재윤(2011). Survival Tourism English, 백산출판사.

문영수 · 천재윤(2011). Contemporary Survival English, 백산출판사.

문영수 · 천재윤(2011). English Heritage for Idioms, Collocations and Phrasal Verbs, 백산출판사.

문영수 · 천재윤(2012). Grammar Free Zone 개정증보, 백산출판사.

천재윤(2006). 술술 내려 읽는 미국영어, 백산출판사.

문영수 영문학박사

주요약력

전북대학교 인문대 영어영문학과 졸업
고려대학교 대학원 영어영문학과 졸업(문학석사)
전북대학교 대학원 영어영문학과 졸업(문학박사)
광신대학교 신학대학원 졸업(목회학 석사)
총회신학원 수료
전북대학교 인문대 강사 역임
University of Wisconsin(Madison) 객원교수
현) 호원대학교 관광대학 호텔관광학부 교수
무디교회 담임목사

주요저서

ABC 대학기초영어(학문사, 1999)
Pops English Conversation(학문사, 2002)
누워서 보는 영어(백산출판사, 2005)
크게 웃고 가는 리딩스킬(백산출판사, 2005)
Grammar Free Zone(백산출판사, 2010)
Survival Tourism English(백산출판사, 2011)
Contemporary Survival English(백산출판사, 2011)
English Heritage for Idioms, Collocations and Phrasal Verbs(백산출판사, 2011)
Grammar Free Zone Revised(백산출판사, 2012)
문박사와 천박사의 English Conversation(백산출판사, 2012) 外

주요논문

- 시대를 향한 한 시인의 노력 : 브라우닝의 낙관주의 연구(2008)
- 우울증의 목회 상담적 치유 연구(2009)
- 문학과 우울증에 관한 연구 : 헤밍웨이의 「노인과 바다」(2012) 外

천재윤 사회언어학박사

주요약력

Major / Sociolinguistics
University of Hawaii NICE course(full scholarship)
Chonbuk National University Graduate School(full scholarship)
전) With Me English Academy Representative
Dr. Cheon's English Academy Representative
Win Language Academy Representative
현) Dr. Cheon's English Academy Representative
Chonbuk National Univ. / Howon Univ. Visiting Prof.

주요저서

누워서 보는 영어(백산출판사, 2005)
크게 웃고 가는 리딩스킬(백산출판사, 2005)
술술 내려 읽는 미국영어(백산출판사, 2006)
Grammar Free Zone(백산출판사, 2010)
Survival Tourism English(백산출판사, 2011)
Contemporary Survival English(백산출판사, 2011)
English Heritage for Idioms, Collocations and Phrasal Verbs(백산출판사, 2011)
Grammar Free Zone Revised(백산출판사, 2012)
문박사와 천박사의 English Conversation(백산출판사, 2012) 外

주요논문

- A Sociolinguistic Study of Korean-English Code-Mixing in Korean Popular Songs(2003)
- An Analysis of Greeting Text and User's Consciousness Survey in the University Homepage(2010)
- A Sociolinguistic Study on the Speech Act of 'Gomapseupnida' in Korean(2010)
- A Sociolinguistic Study on 'Thank you' in English Native Speakers(2011)
- A Study on the Expressions of Gratitude in English and Korean–With Reference to Gratitude Situations–(2012) 外

문박사와 천박사의

English Conversation

2012년 8월 20일 초판 1쇄 인쇄
2012년 8월 25일 초판 1쇄 발행

공저자 문 영 수·천 재 윤
발행인 (寅製) 진 욱 상

발행처 백산출판사

서울시 성북구 정릉3동 653-40
등 록 : 1974. 1. 9. 제 1-72호
전 화 : 914-1621, 917-6240
FAX : 912-4438
http://www.ibaeksan.kr
editbsp@naver.com

저자와의 합의하에 인지첩부 생략

값 14,000원
ISBN 978-89-6183-617-3